AF574685

THE TABLES

THE QUEEN'S LINEAGE

from A.D. 495 to the
Silver Jubilee of
Her Majesty Queen Elizabeth II

G. S. P. FREEMAN-GRENVILLE

REX COLLINGS • LONDON • 1977

ACKNOWLEDGEMENTS

Mrs Philip Chester was the first to suggest to my old friend Rex Collings that a reference book of this kind could be useful, and he passed the idea on to me. I am grateful to them both, and to him also for accepting my suggestion that the ruling kings and queens should be illustrated, whenever possible, from their pence. My thanks are also due to Messrs B. A. Seaby, Ltd, for providing the illustrations.

ABBREVIATIONS

ante	before	illeg.	illegitimate(ly)
b.	born	*jure uxoris*	in the right of his wife
c.	*circa*, about	k.	killed
d.	daughter (of)	m.	married
d.	died	*post*	after
dep.	deposed	s.	son (of)
diss.	marriage dissolved	s.	succeeded (to the throne)
div.	divorced	s.p.	without issue
d.s.p.	died without issue	unm.	unmarried

First published in Great Britain by Rex Collings Ltd
69 Marylebone High Street London W1

ISBN 0860860377

Typesetting by Malvern Typesetting Services
Printed in Great Britain by
Holywell Press Oxford

INTRODUCTION

The Silver Jubilee of Her Majesty Queen Elizabeth II celebrates not only the first twenty-five years of the reign of a greatly loved and incomparable lady, but nearly a millennium and a half of a line of monarchs in almost unbroken family succession since 495. In all that long period only six rulers—Sweyn, Canute I, Canute II Hardicanute, Harold I, Harold II, and William I the Conqueror—have not been descended from Cerdic, who led the West Saxons into England in 495; and who, in 519, in the words of one version of the Anglo-Saxon Chronicle, 'undertook the government of the West Saxons. . . . From that day there have reigned the children of the West Saxon kings.' As King of Wessex Cerdic had a sacred character, claiming to be ninth in descent from Woden (or Wotan, or Odin), the German High God of the Sky: in 828, eleven or twelve generations later, Cerdic's successor Egbert received homage as King of all England. At some period before this the sovereign had been given a sacred Christian character by a solemn blessing and coronation: the earliest known ritual is the mid-eighth-century Pontifical of Archbishop Egbert of York. Ever since, oil has been poured on each monarch's head with substantially the same words as those used at the coronation of Queen Elizabeth II in 1953:

> . . . as Solomon was anointed king by Zadok the priest and Nathan the prophet, so be thou anointed, blessed and consecrated Queen over the Peoples, whom the Lord thy God hath given thee to rule and govern. . . .

These words thus span more than a thousand years of monarchy. No other family has such a record. No European country can exhibit so continuous, so vigorous, or so stable a line of monarchy; no other monarchy is so venerable or has proved so adaptable.

The tale of the history of eighty-one sovereigns, from small beginnings in Wessex to the present Headship of the Commonwealth, is longer and more complex than any ordinary person is likely to bear in mind. The object of this book is simply to present the backbone of the story, the lineage of the Kings and Queens who have ruled England, and the Scottish line which, in the person of James VI of Scotland, I of England, united the two thrones. The English royal lineage is shown in ten tables which include the marriages of the monarchs and of their sons and daughters, but thereafter only those of their descendants who have affected the fortunes of the throne. In all cases they have been given the name by which they are most generally known. It has not been thought necessary to include the lineage of members of the peerage who are of royal descent, nor the numerous descendants of Queen Victoria who married into the majority of the royal houses of Europe. These have only been briefly indicated when their earliest ancestor has been mentioned. An exception has been made in Table 10, to show all the descendants of George V. Table 11 shows the lineage of the Kings of Scotland, who, after Malcolm III's marriage in 1068–9 to Saint Margaret, grand-daughter of Edmund II Ironside, were also all descended from Cerdic.

The tables name over 1100 persons, all of whom have been recorded in the index, so that the reader can easily trace any individual whose dates and relationships he may wish to verify. But we can have little idea of people without knowing what they look like. Plainly a work which illustrated all of more than 1100 persons would not only be unmanageable but also too costly to buy. The oldest existing series of royal portraits is the heads on the penny, which Offa of Mercia first minted in 735: our other coins only began to be minted later. For more than a thousand years the most widely known image of English sovereigns has been on the penny, the commonest coin in every man's pocket; and indeed many men and women have lived and died without ever having seen any other image of the sovereign. It has thus seemed fitting, as far as possible, to illustrate all the Kings and ruling Queens of England and Scotland from their portraits on the penny, and this best emphasizes the continuity of the monarchy.

Since the Act of Settlement of 12 June 1701 the royal succession has been regulated by strict primogeniture. The king's male heirs succeed in order, and, failing them, the female heirs: a woman can only succeed in default of male heirs of her father. This has not always been so, and different rules have prevailed at different times. Not infrequently the rules of custom have been far from clear, and their vagueness frequently led to violent conflict. It is necessary to say something about them if the tables are to be understood.

All the tables show first the sons in order of their birth, and then the daughters in their order. The principles of the succession of the Kings of Wessex are unclear (Table 1), the more so because we do not know the relationship of five of the eighteen rulers to the rest. Among the Saxon kings (Table 2) there appears in the third generation a succession of three brothers, albeit the first to die had a son. Saint Edward the Confessor came to the throne not only as his father's son, but at the request of the Witanagemot, or Council of Wise Men: it might seem there was an element of election. The Witanagemot repeated this action after Harold II's death at the battle of Hastings in 1066, when they chose Edgar Atheling, grandson of

Edmund II Ironside. The choice was abortive because William the Conqueror steadily won members of the Witanagemot over to himself. In his succession other principles emerge. He claimed the throne by designation of Edward the Confessor in 1051: the Bayeux Tapestry emphasizes this by showing the future Harold II kneeling to him in homage in 1064. William's wife, Matilda, was a remote descendant of Alfred the Great; and, by blood only, for he was illegitimate, he was the great nephew of Emma, daughter of Richard I, 3rd Duke of Normandy: she married Ethelred the Unready in 1002, and Edward the Confessor was their son: thus both William and his wife were his cousins. Harold II's only claim was the allegation that Edward the Confessor devised the Crown to him when on his death-bed: this the Witanagemot accepted. William's succession in 1035 as Duke of Normandy was by his father's designation and acceptance by the Norman nobility: they had passed over the possible claims of the surviving legitimate male heirs of Richard I, 3rd Duke of Normandy, in favour of the illegitimate William. This was fully in accord with Norman custom. But William's title to England, accepted fully when he was crowned in Westminster Abbey on 25 December 1066, was by right of conquest.

At his death William I appointed his eldest son, Robert, Duke of Normandy, and his second surviving son, William II Rufus, King of England. On William II's death Robert was heir presumptive to England, but the throne was seized successfully by the youngest brother, Henry I. At this stage the possibility of the succession of a woman became an actuality, for Henry I left only a female heir, Matilda. The nearest surviving male of the line was a grandson of the Conqueror, Stephen; and conflict ensued between her supporters and his from 1135 to 1152, when she resigned the Crown to Stephen for his life, but with the provision that her son, later Henry II, should succeed him. Thus, failing a direct male heir, a male heir through a woman might succeed. The problem did not arise again until some 300 years later, in Tudor times.

The Plantagenet successors of Henry II succeeded by male primogeniture from 1154 until 1399, when the heir presumptive was Edmund, 5th Earl of March (see Table 4), whose grandmother, Philippa, Countess of Ulster, had during her life-time been recognized as Richard II's heir presumptive. But on 30 May 1399 Henry IV, a grandson of Edward III in the direct male line, usurped the throne from Richard II: it was the first of a series of actions which led to the Wars of the Roses, a struggle too complicated even to outline here. There were three monarchs of the House of Lancaster (Table 5), and three of the House of York (Table 6). The two houses were ultimately united by Henry VII, a scion of the House of Lancaster, who in 1486 married Elizabeth of York, whose claim as heir of her brother Edward V was indisputable. Henry VII's own claim was tenuous. He was descended from John of Gaunt and Katherine Swynford, whose children were born in adultery. They were legitimatized by statute in 1397 after their parents marriage, but allegedly were debarred from the throne. However this may be, there were heirs of John of Gaunt senior in line to Henry VII in the persons of the royal line of Portugal. Henry VII's claim was based straightforwardly on right of conquest, as William I's had been.

Henry VIII's failure to provide a male heir other than the sickly Edward VI led to his six marriages. Although Mary I and Elizabeth I were declared bastards when the marriages of their respective mothers were annulled, they were nevertheless declared heirs to the throne in that order, failing Edward VI, in 1543. Four years later, when Henry VIII died, his will passed them over as heirs after Edward VI in favour of the descendants of Mary, Henry VII's younger daughter. Henry VII's elder daughter, Margaret, and her descendants were also passed over because she had married James IV of Scotland: it was not thought fitting for the throne to pass to a foreigner, still less to unite the Crowns. The Princess Mary's granddaughter and heir was Lady Jane Grey, who reigned for eleven days in 1553: this was also in accordance with Edward VI's appointment of her as his heir by Letters Patent. She had too little public support to make good her claim. In the event, following Elizabeth I's death in 1603, James VI of Scotland ascended the English throne as heir to Margaret, Henry VII's elder daughter. His claim was ratified by Parliament in 1604.

The seventeenth century witnessed the struggle between King and Parliament which Parliament so decisively won: it was Parliament which recognized James VI and I's claim, for all his belief in the Divine Right of Kings. It was Parliament, by rebellion, that fought the war that led to Charles I's deposition and execution: it was Parliament which restored Charles II with the support of the army: it was Parliament that proclaimed William III and Mary II as joint rulers on 13 February 1689, having presumed James II's abdication, and which denied the throne to his son the Old Pretender and the subsequent Stewarts of his line: it was Parliament that regulated the succession in the House of Hanover in 1701, following Queen Anne's failure to produce an heir, all her many children having died in infancy. Since then only has succession to the throne followed the strict rule of primogeniture, prescribing the succession of females in default of male heirs. It was Parliament also that in 1936 accepted Edward VIII's abdication after his determination to contract a marriage which did not commend itself to the nation.

The Scottish monarchy followed different principles of succession. It arose from the union of the earlier monarchies of the Scots and of the Picts by Kenneth Mac Alpin, first King of Scotland. He was succeeded by his brother Donald: thereafter lines of cousins contested the throne. In theory the king had the right of tanistry, by which he might nominate his successor, or tanistair. In practice, as Table 11 shows, this system, or lack thereof, led to frequent conflict and assassination. The great crisis arose after Alexander III's death on 19 March 1285–6: his heir was his granddaughter, the two-year-old Margaret, 'The Maid of Norway', who died at sea on the way to Scotland on 26 September 1290. The principal claimants were John Baliol and Robert Bruce, Lord of Annandale, but there were no less than ten other contestants, whose names are marked in Table 11. Many of these claims were wholly speculative. As arbitrator, Edward I of England nominated John Baliol, who was deposed after four years in 1296. Scotland was virtually a province of England until the tide turned in favour of King Robert I the Bruce, grandson of the Lord of Annandale, who was crowned at Scone on 27 March 1306. This act provided a focus for the revival of Scottish nationalism, which was successfully vindicated by Robert I the Bruce at the battle of Bannockburn on 24 June 1314. His grandson Robert II succeeded in the right of his mother, Marjorie, daughter of Robert I the Bruce, who had married Walter the Stewart, 6th High Stewart of Scotland. His successors ruled as Kings of the House of Stewart thereafter. Of these only one was a woman, the tragic Mary, Queen of Scots. Her son James VI's accession to the throne of England as James I in 1603 united the Crowns in one person, but not the two countries. Such a union was attempted under Cromwell, but did not come into effect until the Act of Union of 1706 was passed by the two Parliaments, which united the two kingdoms as the Kingdom of Great Britain, becoming effective when the two Parliaments met together on 1 May 1707.

1 Kings of Wessex

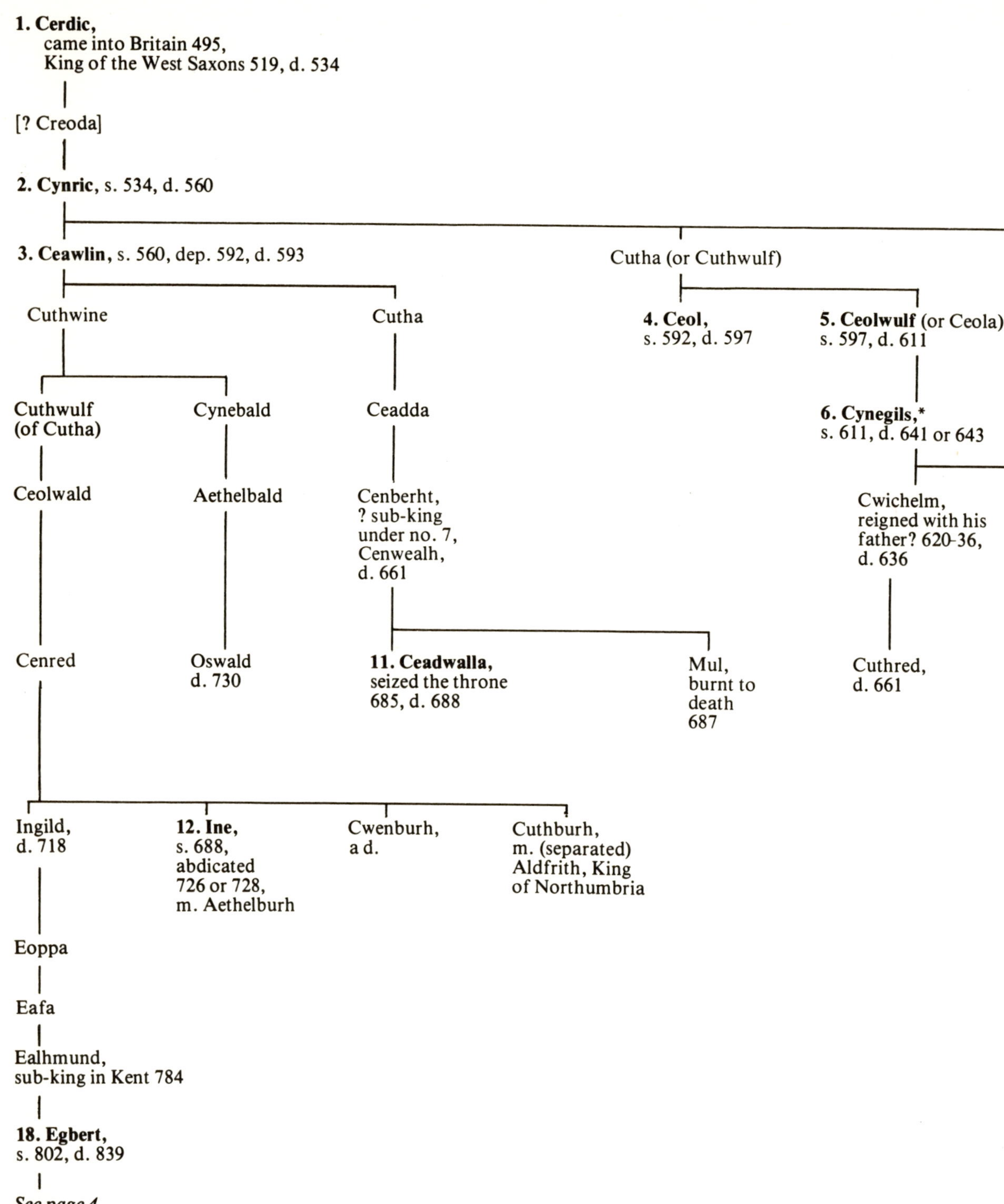

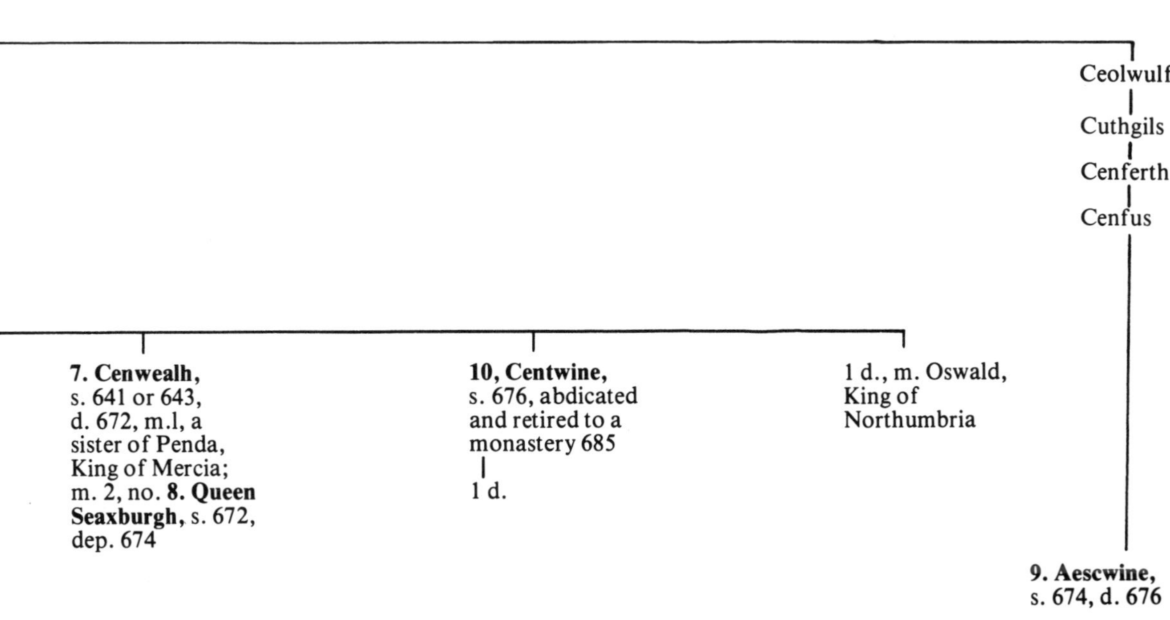

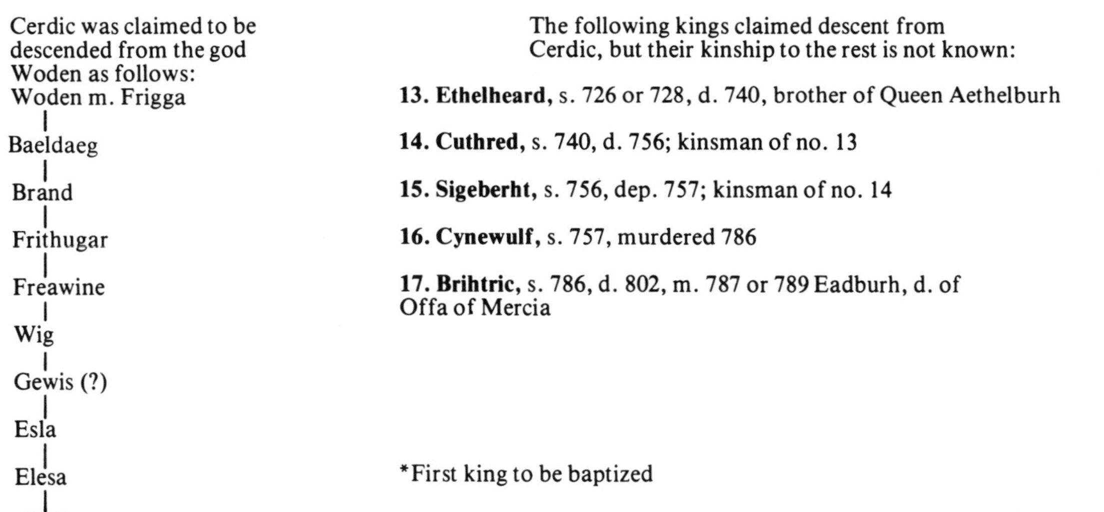

The following kings claimed descent from Cerdic, but their kinship to the rest is not known:

13. Ethelheard, s. 726 or 728, d. 740, brother of Queen Aethelburh

14. Cuthred, s. 740, d. 756; kinsman of no. 13

15. Sigeberht, s. 756, dep. 757; kinsman of no. 14

16. Cynewulf, s. 757, murdered 786

17. Brihtric, s. 786, d. 802, m. 787 or 789 Eadburh, d. of Offa of Mercia

*First king to be baptized

2 Saxon Kings

continued from page 3

1. Egbert, King of Wessex 802, King of England 828, d. 4 Feb. 839

2. Ethelwulf, s. 4 Feb. 839, d. 13 Jan. 855,
m.1, Osburgh (d. 852), d. of Oslac, his Cup Bearer; m.2, 1 Oct. 853, Judith, d. of Charles II, King of France, Holy Roman Emperor

3. Ethelbald†
s. 13 Jan. 855, d. 20 Dec. 860, incestuously m. 855 his stepmother Judith. (She m. 3rd Baldwin I, Count of Flanders.)

4. Ethelbert, s. 20 Dec. 860, d. 866, wife unknown

- Adhelm, d.s.p.
- Ethelward, unsuccessfully claimed the throne, 900; k. in battle of Holme 905, s.p.

5. Ethelred I, s. 866, d. 23 Apr. 871, wife unknown. D.s.p. of wounds in battle of Horton against the Danes

- issue

m.1. Egwina (? his mistress)

- 8. **Athelstan,** s. 4 Sept. 925, d. unm. s.p. 27 Oct. 939
- Alfred, d.s.p.
- Edith, m. 30 Jan. 925 Sihtric Caoch, King of Northumberland, and d. a nun

m.2 (or 1) Aelflaeda, d. of Earl Ethelhelm

- Ethelward, d. 1 Aug. 924
- Edwin, put to death 933
- 2ds—nuns

† No mint

* No portrait on coins

1. Egbert

2. Ethelwulf

4. Ethelbert

5. Ethelred I

6. Alfred the Great

7. *Edward the Elder*

8. *Athelstan*

9. *Edmund I*

10. *Edred*

6. Alfred the Great, b.c. 848, s. 23 Apr. 871, d. 25 Oct. 899, m. 868 Ealswith (d. a nun 904), d. of Ethelred Mucel, Ealdorman of Gaini, and Eadburh, of Mercia

Aethelswith
m. Burgred, King of Mercia

. **Edward the Elder,**
, 25 Oct. 899,
. 17 July 925

Ethelward,
b.c. 880,
d. 26 Oct. 922
3 s.

Elfleda,
m. 886
Ethelred,
Earl of
Mercia

Ethelswithe,
m. Baldwin II,
Count of
Flanders
(d. 917),
d. 7 June 829
issue—from whom descended Matilda, wife of **22. William I the Conqueror**

Ethelgiva,
Abbess of
Shaftesbury

m. 3 (or 2) Eadgifu, d. of Sigehelm, ealdorman of Kent

)giva,
ı. 917
:harles III
he Simple
f France
d. 929),
aving
ssue; m.
, c. 951,
Herbert III,
Count of
Vermandois
nd Troyes
d. 993), and
ad issue

Eadhilda,
m.c. 927
Hugh, Duke
of France,
d.s.p. *ante*
938

Edith,
m. 930
Otto the
Great,
Duke of
Saxony,
Holy
Roman Emperor,
(d. 973), d.
947 leaving
issue

Edgiva,
m. Eberhard
Count of
Nordgau
(d.c. 960)

9. Edmund I
(the Magnificent) b. 921,
s. 27 Oct. 940,
murdered 26
May 946, m.
940 Edgira

10. Edred,
s. 26 May
946, d. 23
Nov. 955
issue

Edgive,
m. (?)
Conrad,
King of
Transjuranian
Burgundy

Edburga,
a nun

11. Edwy the Fair,* b. 941, s. 23 Nov. 955, d. 1 Oct. 959, m. (annulled) a cousin, Elgifa, d.s.p.

12. Edgar the Pacific,*
b.c. 944, usurped Kingdom of Mercia 957, s. 1 Oct. 959, d. 8 July 975

d., name unknown, m. Baldwin, Count of Hesdin

m.1, 961, Ethelfleda, parentage unknown (d. 962)

13. Saint Edward the Martyr, b.c. 963, s. 8 July 975, murdered by his stepmother Queen Elfrida 18 March 979 near Corfe Castle s.p.

m. 2
Wulfthryth

Edith,
Abbess
of
Wilton

m. 3, 964, Elfrida (d. a nun), widow of Earl Ethelwald and d. of Ordgar, ealdorman of Devon

Edmund,
Atheling,
d.s.p.c.
972

14. Ethelred II
See page 6

* No portrait on coins

13. *Edward the Martyr*

continued from page 5

14. Ethelred II the Redeless[1]
b.c. 966, s. 18 March 979, fled to Normandy 1013, restored 1014, murdered 23 Apr. 1016

m.1, 984, Elgiva (d. 1002), d. of Earl Thorold of Northumbria

m. 2. 1002, Emma, d. of Richard I, 3rd Duke of Normandy (see Table 3); she m. 2, **Canute I** (see 2A)

Issue of m. 1:

- Athelstan, b. 986, k. in battle against the Danes 1011, unm.
- Egbert
- **16. Edmund II Ironside,**† b.c. 989, s. 23 Apr. 1016, murdered 30 Nov. 1016, m. 1015 Algitha, widow of Sigfrid, a Danish nobleman
  - Edmund, b. 1016, m. Agatha, d. of Saint Stephen I of Hungary, d.s.p.
  - Edward the Exile, b. posthumously 1017, d. 1057, m. Agatha, d. of Conrad II of Franconia, Holy Roman Emperor
    - Edgar Atheling, b. 1053, d. unm. *post* 1125, chosen King of England by the Witanagemot on the death of Harold II
    - Saint Margaret, m. 1068 as his 2nd wife Malcolm III, King of Scotland (see Table 11, no. 19) and d. 16 Nov. 1093 leaving issue
    - Christina, Abbess of Romsey, d. unm.
- Eadred
- Edwy, 3d. murdered 1017

Issue of m. 2:

- **20. Saint Edward the Confessor,** elected King of England by the Witanagemot 1042, d.s.p. 5 Jan. 1066, having left as his heir William, 7th Duke of Normandy, his cousin by blood, m. 23 Jan. 1045 Edith (or Eadgyth), d. of Godwin, Earl of Wessex (see 2B)
- Alfred, blinded by Earl Godwin, d. in prison 1035
- Goda, m.1, Drog[o] Count of Amiens and Vexin and had issue, m. 2, Eustac[e] Count of Boulogne (d. 1093), without further issue

† No mint

14. Ethelred II

20. Edward the Confessor

1. Commonly known as 'The Unready'. His nickname 'The Redeless' in fact means that he attempted to rule without the advice of his council.

2A Kings of the House of Denmark

15. Sweyn,† King of Denmark and Norway from 985, usurper, proclaimed King of England by right of conquest 1013, d. 3 Feb. 1014, m. Gunhilda, (d.c. 1015) d. of Mieszko, Duke of Poland

Harold III, King of Denmark 1014, deposed by his brother Canute 1016, d. 1017

17. Canute I, b.c. 995, King of Denmark and England, contested the throne of England on the death of his father 1014, received Mercia, E. Anglia and Northumbria by treaty, seized the throne of England 1016, King of Norway by right of conquest 1030-35, d. 12 Nov. 1035,

Thyra, b. 994, m. as his first wife Godwin, Earl of Wessex (see below 2B), and d.c. 1018, leaving issue

m.1, Aelgifu (whom he repudiated) (d. 31 Dec. 1044), d. of Elfhelm, Earl of Northampton

m. 2, 1017, Emma, widow of **Ethelred II** (see above, no. 14)

Sweyn, King of Norway, d. 1036

18. Harold I Harefoot, King of England, s. 12 Nov. 1035, d. unm. s.p. 17 March 1040 (cf. 18)

19. Canute II Hardicanute, b. 1018, King of Denmark 1035, s. as King of England 17 March 1040, d. unm. s.p. 8 June 1042

Cunigunda, m. 10 June 1036 Henry III of Franconia, Holy Roman Emperor, d. 18 July 1038, leaving issue

† No mint

17. Canute I

18. Harold I

19. Canute II

21. Harold II

2B King of the House of Godwin

Godwin, Earl of Wessex (d. 15 Apr. 1053), son of Wulfnoth, descent unknown, m. 2, Gythe, a relative of King Canute I, at whose court he was an influential nobleman

21. Harold II, b.c. 1022, Earl of Wessex 1053, usurped the throne 7 Jan. 1066, k. at Hastings 14 Oct. 1066, leaving 4s. 2d.

Edith (or Eadgyth), d. 19 Dec. 1075, m. 23 Jan. 1045 **Saint Edward the Confessor**—see Table 2, no. 20

3 Dukes of Normandy and Norman Kings of England

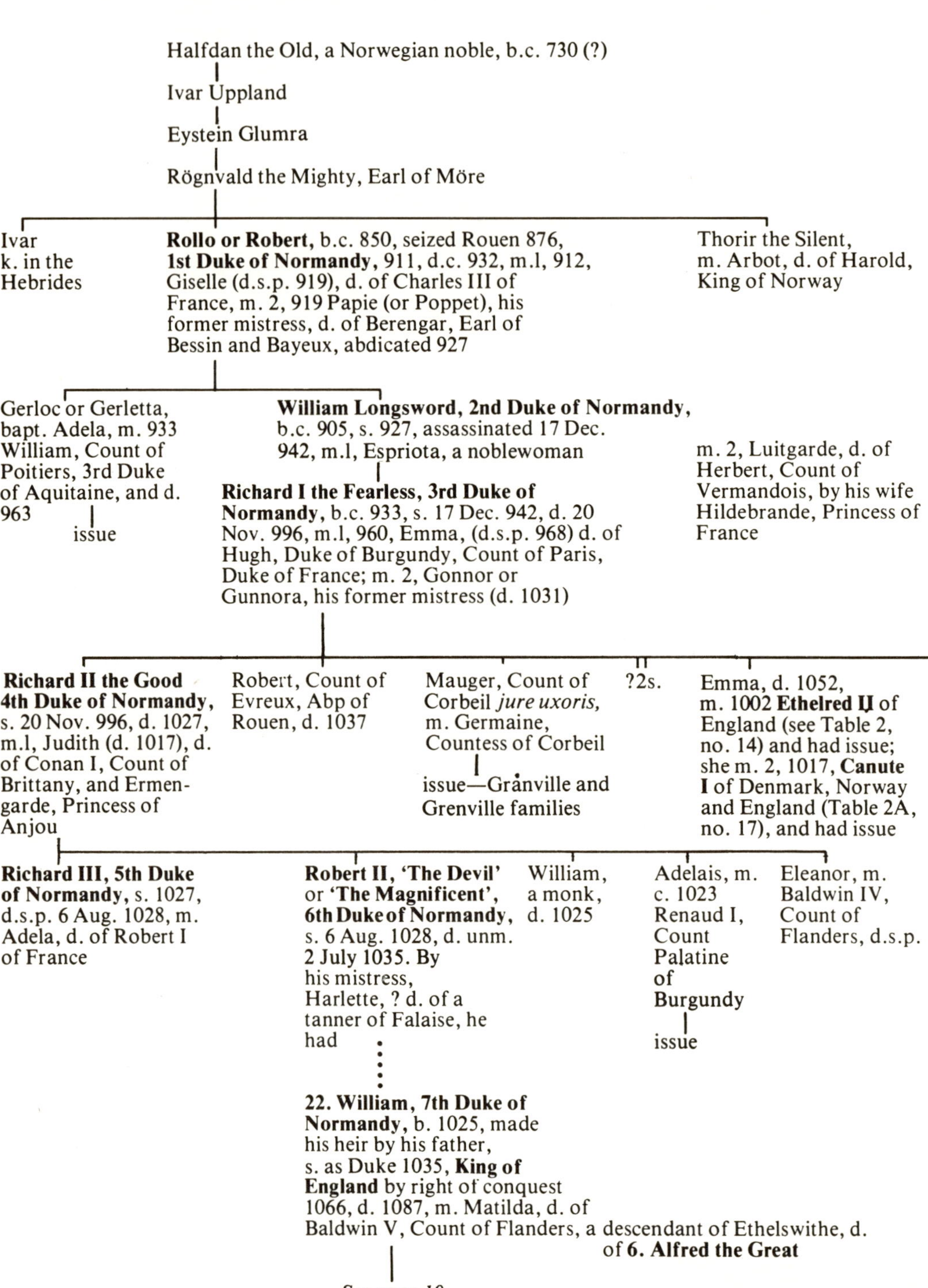

See page 10

22. William I the Conqueror

Hawise, m. Geoffrey I, Count of Brittany, d. 1034
issue

Maud (or Matilda), m. Eudes, Count of Blois, Chartres and Troyes, d.s.p. 1017

Beatrice, m. Ebles, Viscount of Turenne

Duke **Richard II,** m. 2, Margaret, d. of **Sweyn,** King of Denmark, Norway and England, d.s.p.

Duke **Richard II,** m. 3, Papie, of unknown parentage

William, Count of Arques, m. a d. of Hugh, Count of Ponthieu. Claimed Duchy of Normandy in 1035 as legitimate heir of Duke Robert II

Mauger, a monk, Abp of Rouen, d.c. 1055

†Harlette, mistress of Duke **Robert II,** m. later Harlevin, Seigneur de Conteville

Odo, Bp of Bayeux, Earl of Kent, Regent of England, d. 1096

Robert, Count of Mortain, d. 1091

Adelaide, m. Waltheof, Earl of Huntingdon

Matilda, Countess of Huntingdon, m.1, Simon de Senlis or St Liz; m. 2, c. 1114, David I, King of Scotland

subsequent Kings of Scotland

(See page 31)

continued from page 8

Robert III, 8th Duke of Normandy, b. 1051, d. 1134, m. Sybilla (d. 1103), d. of Geoffrey, Count of Conversano

issue

Richard, Duke of Bernay, b.c. 1054, d. 1081

23. William II Rufus, b. 1056, s. 9 Sept. 1087 by designation of his father, d. unm., k. hunting in the New Forest 2 Aug. 1100

24. Henry I, b. 1070, usurped the throne from his brother Robert 2 Aug. 1100, d. 1 Dec. 1135; m.1, Matilda (Eadgith) (b. 1079, d. 1 May 1118), d. of Malcolm III of Scotland (see Table 11, no. 19), great-grand-daughter of Edmund II Ironside (see Table 2, no. 16); he m. 2, 2 Feb. 1121, Adela, d. of Godfrey, Duke of Lower Lorraine, d.s.p.

Cecilia, b.c. 1055, d. 1127, Abbess of Caen

William. 10th Duke of Normandy, b. 1101, m. 1119 Isabella, d. of Fulk of Anjou, King of Jerusalem, d.s.p. 26 Nov. 1119, drowned in the *White Ship*

Richard, d. unm., drowned in the *White Ship* 26 Nov. 1119

26. Matilda, Queen of England, b. 1103, recognized heir presumptive 1119, d. 1167, m.1, Henry V of Franconia, Holy Roman Emperor (d. 1125); m. 2, 1127, Geoffrey V Plantagenet, Count of Anjou, Duke of Normandy (d. 1150) (see Table 4); proclaimed Queen Apr. 1141, but never crowned; renounced claim in favour of her cousin **25. Stephen** 1152, for his life, with remainder to her son **27. Henry II**

27. Henry II, King of England 1154-89: see Table 4: House of Anjou or Plantagenets

See page 12

Geoffrey VI, Count of Anjou and Nantes, b. 1 June 1134, d. unm. 1157

William, Count of Poitou, b. Aug. 1136, d. unm. 1164

Emma, m. 1173 David (d. 1204), s. of Owen Gwynedd, Prince of North Wales

issue

23. William II

24. Henry I

25. Stephen

26. Matilda

Adelaide, formally betrothed to Harold II, King of England (see Table 2B), d. unm. 1065

Matilda, d. unm.

Constance, b. 1061, m. 1068 Alain V, Count of Brittany, d.s.p. 1090

Adela, b.c. 1062, d. (a nun) 1137, m. 1080 Stephen (or Henry) Count of Blois and Chartres (k. 1102)

Agatha, d. unm. c. 1080

25. Stephen, b.c. 1096, usurped England and Normandy from his cousin **26. Matilda** 1135; lost Normandy 1144; d. 25 Oct. 1154; m.c. 1123 Matilda, Countess of Mortain and Boulogne, d. of Eustace II, Count of Boulogne and his wife Mary, d. of Malcolm III of Scotland (see Table 11, no. 19)

5s. 1d.

Baldwin, b.c. 1124, d.c. 1135

Eustace IV, Count of Boulogne, b.c. 1127, d.s.p. 1152, m. Constance, d. of Louis VI, King of France

William II, Count of Mortain and Boulogne, b.c. 1137, d.s.p. 1159, m.c. 1149 Isabel, d. of William de Warenne, Earl of Surrey. K. in battle

Matilda, b. 1134, d.c. 1137

Mary, Countess of Mortain and Boulogne, b. 1136, d.s.p., a nun, 1182, m. Matthew I, Count of Alsace

4 The House of Anjou or Plantagenets

Geoffrey V, 10th Count of Anjou and Count of Maine (1129), Duke of Normandy 1144-9, when he ceded it to his son, Henry II, b. 24 Aug. 1113, d. 11 Sept. 1150, m. 3 Apr. 1127 **26. Matilda**, Queen of England. With other issue (see Table 3, no. 26) they had

27. Henry II, b. 5 March 1133, s. his mother's cousin **25. Stephen** 25 Oct. 1154, Duke of Normandy by cession from his father 1149, Duke of Aquitaine *jure uxoris* 1152, d. 6 July 1189, m. Whitsun 1152 Eleanor (d. 26 Jan. 1202), div. wife of Louis VII, King of France, d. of William, Count of Poitou

William, b. 17 Aug. 1152, d. 1156

Henry, Duke of Normandy and Count of Anjou, b. 25 Feb. 1155, crowned King of England 15 July 1170 during the reign of his father, d.s.p. 11 June 1183, m. 1173 Margaret, d. of Louis VII, King of France. She m. 2 Bela, King of Hungary, and d. 1198

28. Richard I, Coeur de Lion, b. 8 Sept. 1157, s. 6 July 1189, d.s.p. 6 Apr. 1199, m. 12 May 1191 Berengaria (b.c. 1163, d.c. 1230), d. of Sancho IV, King of Navarre, and k. at siege of Chalus

Geoffrey, Duke of Brittany, b. 23 Sept. 1158, d. 19 Aug. 1186, m. July 1181 Constance, d. and heir of Conan IV, Duke of Brittany and Earl of Richmond (d. 31 Aug. 1201)

- Arthur, Duke of Brittany, b. posthumously 29 March 1187, d. unm., k. 3 Apr. 1203, on whom the right to the throne devolved on the death of his uncle, **Richard I**
- Eleanor, b. 1184, d. unm. 10 Aug. 1241

---

31. Edward I, b. 17 June 1239, s. 16 Nov. 1272, d. 8 July 1307, m. 1, Oct. 1254 Eleanor (d. 28 Nov. 1290), d. of Ferdinand III, King of Castile

Edmund, Earl of Lancaster and Derby (Crouchback), King of Sicily, b. 16 Jan. 1245, d. 5 June 1296, m.1 Aveline (d.s.p. 10 Nov. 1273), d. of William, Count of Aumale; m. 2, *ante* 3 Feb. 1275-6 Blanche (d. 2 May 1302), widow of Henry I, King of Navarre, d. of Robert I, Count of Artois
issue

Richard, b.c. 1247, d. *ante* 1256

John, b.c. 1250, d. *ante* 1256

William, b. and d. c. 1250

Henry, d. young

Children of Edward I:

John, b. 10 July 1266, d. 1 Aug. 1272

Henry, b. 1268, d.c. 14 Oct. 1274

Alphonso, b. 24 Nov. 1273, d. 19 Aug. 1284

32. Edward II, b. 25 Apr. 1284, created 1st Prince of Wales 7 Feb. 1301-2, s. 8 July 1307, d. 7 Jan. 1327, m. 28 Jan. 1308 Isabella (d. 22 Aug. 1358), d. of Philip IV, King of France; dep. 7 Jan. 1327 and murdered at Berkeley Castle, 21 Sept. 1327
issue—*see page 14*

Eleanor (1), b. 1264, d. 1298, m.1, 15 Aug. 1282, Alphonso, Prince of Aragon (d. 1282); m. 2, 20 Sept. 1293, Henry III, Count of Bar
issue

Joan, b. 1272, d. 23 Apr. 1307, m. 1, 2 May 1290, Gilbert de Clare, Earl of Gloucester, (d. 7 Dec. 1295); m. 2, 1297, Ralph de Monthermer, Lord Monthermer
issue

27. Henry II

28. Richard I

29. John

30. Henry III

31. Edward I

32. Edward II

29. John, b. 24 Dec. 1166, s. 6 Apr. 1199, d. 19 Oct. 1216, m.l., 1189, Isabel, d. of William, Earl of Gloucester (annulled 1200); m.2, 24 Aug. 1200, Isabella, d. and heir of Aymer de Valence, Count of Angoulême (d. 31 May 1246)

Maud, b. 1156, d. 8 June 1189, m. Henry the Lion, Duke of Saxony
issue

Eleanor, b. 13 Oct. 1162, d. 31 Oct. 1214, m. Sept. 1177 Alfonso VIII, King of Castile
issue

Joan, b. Oct. 1165, d. a nun 4 Sept. 1199, m.l, 13 Feb. 1177, William II, King of Sicily (d. 18 Nov. 1189), and had issue; she m. 2, Oct. 1196, Raymond, Count of Toulouse (d. 1222), having further issue

30. Henry III, b. 10 Oct. 1206, s. 19 Oct. 1216, d. 16 Nov. 1272, m. 14 Jan. 1236 Eleanor, (d. a nun 24 June 1291), d. of Raymond Berengar IV, Count of Provence

Richard, Earl of Cornwall, b. 5 Jan. 1208, d. 2 Apr. 1272, elected King of the Romans 17 May 1257, m.l, 30 March 1231, Isabel (d. 19 Jan. 1240), d. of William Marshal, Earl of Pembroke, and had issue; he m.2, 23 Nov. 1243, Sanchia, d. of Raymond Berengar IV, Count of Provence and had issue; he m. 3, 1269, Beatrice, d. of Theodoric von Falkestein, without issue

Joan, b. 22 July 1210, d.s.p. 4 March 1237-8, m. Alexander II of Scotland (see Table 11, no. 28)

Isabella, b. 1214, d. 1 Dec. 1241, m. 20 July 1235 Frederick II, Holy Roman Emperor
issue

Eleanor, b. 1215, d. 13 Apr. 1275, m.l, 23 Apr. 1224, William Marshal, Earl of Pembroke (d.s.p. 15 Apr. 1231); m.2, 7 Jan. 1238-9, Simon de Montfort (k. in battle of Evesham, 4 Aug. 1265)
issue

Margaret, b. 5 Oct. 1240, d. 27 Feb. 1274, m. Alexander III of Scotland—see Table 11, no. 29
issue

Beatrix, b. 25 June 1242, d. 24 March 1275, m. 22 Jan. 1260 John II de Dreux, Duke of Brittany and Earl of Richmond (d. 18 Nov. 1305)
issue

King Edward I, m.2, 8 Sept. 1299, Margaret (d. 14 Feb. 1317), d. of Philip III, King of France

Margaret, b. 11 Sept. 1275, d. 1318, m. 9 July 1290 John II, Duke of Brabant (d. 27 Oct. 1312)
issue

Mary, b. 22 Apr. 1279, d.a nun c. 1332

Elizabeth, b. Aug. 1282, d.5 May 1316, m.l, 8 Jan. 1296, John I, Count of Holland (d.s.p. 10 Nov. 1299); m.2, Humphrey de Bohun, Earl of Hereford and Essex
issue

Thomas of Brotherton, Earl of Norfolk, b. 1 June 1300, d. Aug. 1338, m.l, Alice, d. of Sir Roger Hayles, and had issue; m.2, Mary de Braose (d. 9 June 1362), widow of Sir Ralph de Cobham, s.p.

Edmund of Woodstock, Earl of Kent, b. 5 Aug. 1301, beheaded 19 March 1330, m. Margaret (d. 29 Sept. 1349), widow of John Comyn of Badenoch, d. of John, Lord Wake of Lyell
issue inc. Joan, the Fair Maid of Kent, who m. Edward the Black Prince

Eleanor (2), b. 1306, d. in infancy

continued from page 12

33. Edward III, b. 13 Nov. 1312, s. 7 Jan. 1327, d. 22 June 1377, m. 24 Jan. 1329 Philippa (d. 15 Aug. 1369), d. of William III, Count of Holland and Hainault

John, Earl of Cornwall, b. 25 Aug. 1316, d. unm. 14 Sept. 1336

Eleanor, b. 1318, d. 22 Apr. 1355, m. 1332 Reynald II, Duke of Gueldres (d. 12 Oct. 1343)
- issue

Joan, b. 1321, d.s.p. 7 Sept. 1362, m. 17 July 1328 David II, King of Scotland—see Table 11, no. 33

Children of Edward III:

Edward, 'The Black Prince', Prince of Wales, b. 15 June 1330, d. 8 June 1376, m. 10 Oct. 1361 his cousin Joan, 'The Fair Maid of Kent', d. of his step great-uncle Edmund, Earl of Kent (see above)

William of Hatfield, b. 1336, d. young

Lionel of Antwerp, Duke of Clarence, b. 29 Nov. 1338, d. 17 Oct. 1368, m.1, Elizabeth de Burgh, Countess of Ulster (d. 1363), d. and heir of William, 3rd Earl of Ulster; he m. 2, 28 May 1368, Violante (d.s.p.c. 1404), d. of Galeazzo II Visconti, Lord of Milan

John of Gaunt, Duke of Lancaster—see Table 5—House of Lancaster, pp. 16-17

Children of Edward, 'The Black Prince':

Edward of Angoulême, b. 27 July 1364; d. 1372

34. Richard II, (Richard of Bordeaux), b. 6 Jan. 1366, s. 22 June 1377, dep. 30 Sept. 1399, murdered 14 Feb. 1400 s.p., m.1, Anne (d. 7 June 1394), d. of Charles IV, Holy Roman Emperor; m. 2, 1396, Isabel (d. 13 Sept. 1409) d. of Charles VI, King of France

Child of Lionel of Antwerp:

Philippa, Countess of Ulster, heir presumptive to King Richard II, b. 16 Aug. 1355, d. 5 Jan. 1377-8, m. 1368 Edmund Mortimer, 3rd Earl of March (d. 27 Dec. 1381)

Children of Philippa:

Roger Mortimer, 4th Earl of March, b. 1 Sept. 1373, k. in battle 20 July 1398, declared heir to the throne 1377, m. Eleanor, d. of Thomas Holand, Earl of Kent

1s. 3d.

Children of Roger Mortimer:

Edmund, 5th Earl of March, heir presumptive of England, b. 6 Nov. 1391, d.s.p. 19 Jan. 1424-5, m. Anne (d. 20 Sept. 1432), d. of 5th Earl of Stafford

Roger, d.s.p.c. 1412

Anne, b. 27 Jan. 1390, d. Sept. 1411, m.c. May 1406 Richard, Earl of Cambridge —issue—see Table 6, p. 18

Eleanor, b.c. 1395, m. c. 1408 Edward, Lord Courtenay, d.s.p.

33. Edward III

34. Richard II

Edmund of Langley, Duke of York—see Table 6—House of York, pp. 18–19	Thomas of Woodstock, 1st Duke of Gloucester, b. 7 Jan. 1355–6, murdered at Calais 8 Sept. 1397, m. *post* 1374 Eleanor (d. a nun 2 Oct. 1399), d. of Humphrey de Bohun, Earl of Hereford	Isabel, b. 1332, d. 1382, m. 27 July 1365 1st Earl of Bedford (d. 8 Feb. 1396–7)	Joan, b. 1335, d. 2 Sept. 1348	Blanche, b. 1342, d. in infancy	Mary, b. 10 Oct. 1344, d.s.p. 1362, m. 1361 John V, Duke of Brittany and Earl of Richmond	Margaret, b. 20 July 1346, d.s.p. 1361, m. 1359 John Hastings, 2nd Earl of Pembroke (d. 16 Apr. 1375)
	issue	issue				

5 The House of Lancaster

John of Gaunt, Duke of Lancaster, King of Castile and León, b. 24 June 1340, d. 3 Feb. 1399, m.1, 19 May 1359 Blanche (d. 31 Sept. 1369), d. and heir of Henry, 1st Duke of Lancaster, great-grand-daughter of King Henry III

35. Henry IV, b. 30 May 1366, usurped the throne from Richard II 30 Sept. 1399, d. 21 March 1413, m.1, 1380, Lady Mary de Bohun (b. 1370, d. 4 July 1394), d. of Humphrey, Earl of Hereford; he m. 2, 7 Feb. 1403, Joanne (d. 10 June 1437), widow of John V de Montfort, Duke of Brittany, d. of Charles, King of France, without issue

Philippa, b. 31 March 1360, d. 9 June 1415, m. 11 Feb. 1386 John I, King of Portugal

issue—Kings of Portugal

Elizabeth, b. 1362, d. 24 Nov. 1425, m.1, 24 June 1380 (annulled), John Hastings, Earl of Pembroke; m. 2, 1384 John Holand, Duke of Exeter (beheaded 9 Jan. 1399-1400)

issue

Isabel, d. young

36. Henry V, b. 9 Aug. 1397, s. 21 March 1413, d. 31 Aug. 1422, m. 3 Jan. 1420 Catherine (b. 1401, d. 3 Jan. 1437), d. of Charles VI, King of France: she m. 1428 Owen ap Meredith Tudor and was grandmother of King Henry VII—see Table 7

37, 39. Henry VI, b. 6 Dec. 1421, s. 31 Aug. 1422, dep. by Edward IV 4 May 1461 (see Table 6, 38, 40); restored 9 Oct. 1470, again dep. Apr. 1471, d.c. 21 May 1471, m. 22 Apr. 1445 Margaret (d. 25 Aug. 1482), d. of René, Duke of Anjou

Edward, Prince of Wales, b. 13 Oct. 1453, k. at battle of Tewkesbury 4 May 1471, m. Aug. 1470 Lady Anne Nevill (b.c. 1454, d. 16 March 1485), d. and co-heir of Richard, Earl of Warwick; she m. 2, King Richard III (Table 6, no. 42)

Thomas, Duke of Clarence, b.c. May 1388, k. at battle of Baugé 22 March 1421, m. 1411 Margaret (d. c. Dec. 1439), widow of John Beaufort, 1st Earl of Somerset, d. of Thomas Holand, 2nd Earl of Kent

John, Duke of Bedford, Regent of France during Henry VI's minority, b. 20 June 1389, d.s.p. 15 Sept. 1435, m.1, 17 Apr. 1423, Anne (d. 14 Nov. 1432), d. of John, Duke of Burgundy; m. 2, 20 Apr. 1433, Jaquetta (d. 30 May 1472), d. of Peter of Luxembourg

Humphrey, Duke of Gloucester, b. 3 Oct. 1390, d.s.p. 23 Feb. 1447, m.1, Jacqueline, Countess of Holland and Hainault (annulled c. 1430); m. 2, c. 1430, Eleanor (d. 1454), d. of Richard, 2nd Lord Cobham

Blanche, b. 1392, d. 21 May 1409, m. 1402 Louis III, Elector Palatine

issue

Philippa, b. 1393, d. 5 Jan. 1430, m. 26 Oct. 1406 Eric, King of Denmark (d. 1459) s.p.

35. Henry IV

36. Henry V

37, 39. Henry VI

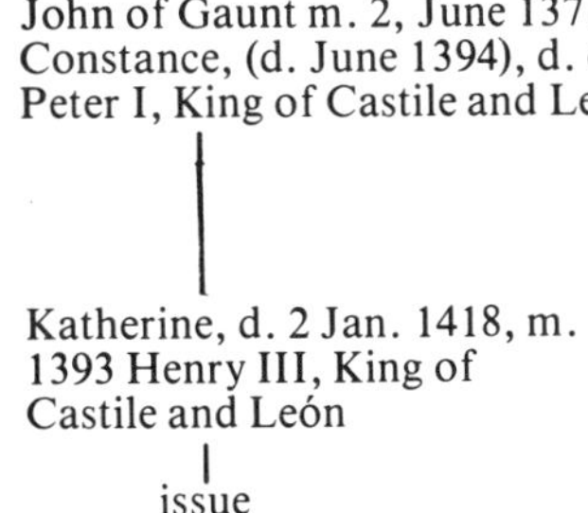

John of Gaunt m. 2, June 1371, Constance, (d. June 1394), d. of Peter I, King of Castile and León

Katherine, d. 2 Jan. 1418, m. 1393 Henry III, King of Castile and León

issue

John of Gaunt m. 3, 1396–7, his former mistress Katherine (d. 10 May 1403), widow of Sir Hugh Swynford, and d. of Sir Payn Roët. Their children were born in adultery, and surnamed Beaufort, and although legitimatized by Statute 20 Richard III (1397) were allegedly debarred from the throne. The eldest son

John, Earl of Somerset, Marquess of Dorset, b. c. 1372, d. 16 March 1410, m.c. 1399 Margaret, d. of Thomas Holand, 2nd Earl of Kent, s. of Joan, 'The Fair Maid of Kent', d. of Edmund of Woodstock, Earl of Kent—see Table 4

Henry, 2nd Earl of Somerset, b. 25 Nov. 1400, d. unm. 25 Nov. 1418

John, 3rd Earl and Duke of Somerset, b. 25 March 1404, d. 27 May 1444, m. Margaret (d. 8 Aug. 1482), d. of John Beauchamp, Lord Beauchamp of Bletso

Margaret ('The Lady Margaret'), b. Apr. 1441, d. 5 July 1509, m.1, 1455, Edmund Tudor (d. 1 Nov. 1456), 1st Earl of Richmond, s. of Owen ap Meredith Tudor and Catherine, widow of King Henry V

43. Henry VII—see Table 7—House of Tudor

Thomas, Earl of Perche, b. 1405, d. unm. 1432

Edmund, Marquess of Dorset, Duke of Somerset, b. 1406, k. 22 May 1455 at battle of St Alban's, m. Eleanor (d. 12 March 1467), widow of Thomas, 9th Baron de Ros, d. of Richard Beauchamp, 2nd Earl of Warwick and Albemarle

issue

2d.

6 The House of York

Edmund of Langley, Duke of York (see Table 4 above), b. 5 June 1341, d. 1 Aug. 1402, m.1, March 1371-2, Isabel (d. 23 Nov. 1392), d. of Peter, King of Castile and León; he m. 2, 4 Nov. 1393 Joan, d. of Thomas Holand, Earl of Kent, without further issue

Edward, 2nd Duke of York and Duke of Albemarle, b.c. 1373, k. at the battle of Agincourt 25 Oct. 1415, m. Philippa (d.s.p. 17 July 1431), d. of John, 2nd Lord Mohun of Dunster

Richard, Earl of Cambridge, b. 1375, beheaded 5 Aug. 1415, m.1, Anne Mortimer (d. Sept. 1411), d. of Roger, 4th Earl of March; m 2, c. 1411 15, Maud, d. of Thomas, Lord de Clifford (d. 26 Aug. 1446), without further issue

Richard, 3rd Duke of York, heir to the throne on the death of his uncle Edmund Mortimer, 5th Earl of March (see Table 4) and Earl of Ulster, b. 21 Sept. 1411, m. *ante* 18 Oct. 1424 Cecily (d. a nun 31 May 1495), d. of Ralph Nevill, 1st Earl of Westmoreland, k. at the battle of Wakefield 31 Dec. 1460

Constance, d. 28 Nov. 1416, m. 1386, Thomas le Despencer, 1st Earl of Gloucester

Henry of Hatfield, b. 10 Feb, 1440-1, d. young

38, 40. Edward IV, b. 28 Apr. 1442, seized the throne 4 March 1461; dep. 9 Oct. 1470; restored 4 May 1471, d. 9 Apr. 1483, m. 1 May 1464 Elizabeth (b.c. 1437, d. 7 June 1492), d. of Sir Richard Widville (or Woodville), Earl of Rivers, and widow of John Grey, Lord Ferrers

Edmund, Duke of Rutland, b. 17 May 1443, k. at battle of Wakefield 31 Dec. 1460 unm.

George, Duke of Clarence, b. 21 Oct. 1449, murdered 18 Feb. 1477, m. 11 July 1469 Isabel (d. 12 Dec. 1476), d. of Richard Nevill, Earl of Warwick

Edward, Earl of Warwick, b. 21 Feb. 1475, beheaded 24 Nov. 1499, the last male to be born a Plantagenet

Margaret, Countess of Salisbury, b. 14 Aug. 1473, beheaded 27 May 1541, m. 22 Sept. 1494 Sir Richard Pole (d. Nov. 1504). She was the last surviving Plantagenet

41. Edward V,† b. 4 Nov. 1470, s. 9 Apr. 1483, dep. 23 June 1483, and murdered in the Tower of London with his brother, Richard, Duke of York

Richard, Duke of York, b. 17 Aug. 1473, d.c. 23 June 1483, when he was murdered with his brother, Edward V: m. 1477-8 Anne (d.s.p. 16 Jan. 1480-1) d. of John Mowbray, Duke of Norfolk

George, Duke of Bedford, b. March 1476-7, d.c. 1481

Elizabeth ('Elizabeth of York'), b. 11 Feb. 1465, d. 11 Feb. 1502-3, m. **43. Henry VII**—see Table 7; she was heir presumptive to the throne, but not so recognized, on the death of her brothers, Edward V and Richard, Duke of York

†Coins extremely rare: no portrait available

38, 40. Edward IV

42. Richard III

42. Richard III, b. 2 Oct. 1452, seized the throne 23 June 1483, k. at battle of Bosworth Field 22 Aug. 1485, m. 12 July 1472 Lady Anne Nevill, widow of Edward, Prince of Wales (see Table 5) (b.c. 1454, d. 16 March 1485), d. of Richard Nevill, Earl of Warwick | Edward, Prince of Wales, b. 1473, d. 31 March 1484, buried at Sheriff Hutton, York	Anne, b. 10 Aug. 1439, d. 14 Jan. 1475-6, m.1, (annulled 1472) 30 July 1447, Henry Holand, Duke of Exeter (d. 1473), having 1d.; she m. 2, 1472, Sir Thomas Leger, and had 1d.	Elizabeth, b. 22 Apr. 1444, d.c. 1503, m. Oct. 1460 John de la Pole, 2nd Duke of Suffolk | issue	Margaret, b. 3 May 1446, d.s.p. 16 Apr. 1503, m. 9 July 1468, as 3rd wife, Charles the Bold, Duke of Burgundy	Ursula, d. young

Mary, b. Aug. 1466, d. 23 May 1482	Cecily, b. 1469, d.s.p. 24 Aug. 1507, m.1, c. Dec. 1487, John, 1st and last Viscount Welles, (d.s.p. 9 Feb. 1498-9); m. 2, 1503, Thomas Kyme	Margaret, b. 19 Apr. 1472, d. Dec. 1472	Anne, b. 2 Nov. 1475, d.s.p. 23 Nov. 1511, m. 4 Feb. 1494-5 Thomas Howard, 3rd Duke of Norfolk, as his 1st wife	Katherine, b. 1479, d. 15 Nov. 1527, m. Sir William Courtenay, later Earl of Devon (d. 9 June 1511) | issue	Bridget, b. 10 Nov. 1480, d. a nun 1517

7 The House of Tudor

43. Henry VII, b. 28 July 1457, (see Table 6), proclaimed King of England by right of conquest 22 Aug 1485, d. 22 Apr. 1509, m. 18 Jan. 1486 Elizabeth (b. 11 Feb. 1465, d. 11 Feb. 1502-3), eldest d. of Edward IV (see Table 6)

Arthur, Prince of Wales, b. 20 Sept. 1486, d.s.p. 2 Apr. 1502, m. Catherine, Princess of Aragon, (b. 16 Dec. 1485, d. 6 Jan., 1536), d. of Ferdinand V, King of Castile and Aragon; she m. 2 his brother, Henry VIII

44. Henry VIII, b. 28 June 1491, s. 22 Apr. 1509, King of Ireland from 1540-1, d. 28 Jan. 1547, m.1, 11 June 1509, his brother's widow Catherine (marriage diss. 23 May 1533)

Henry, Duke of Cornwall, b. 1 Jan., d. 22 Feb. 1510-11

Duke of Cornwall, b. and d. Nov. 1513

a prince, b. and d. Dec. 1514

47. Mary I, b. 18 Feb. 1515-16, s. 19 July 1553, d.s.p. 17 Nov. 1558, m. 25 July 1554 Philip II,King of Spain, etc., (d. 13 Sept. 1598)

Henry VIII m. 2, 25 Jan. 1532-3, Anne (b. 1501, marriage diss. 17 May 1536, beheaded 19 May 1536), d. of Sir Thomas Boleyn

a son, b. and d. 29 Jan. 1535-6

48. Elizabeth I, b. 7 Sept. 1533, s. 17 Nov. 1558, d. unm. 24 March 1603

Henry VIII m. 3, 20 May 1536, Jane (b.c. 1500, d. 14 Oct. 1537), d. of Sir John Seymour

45. Edward VI, b. 12 Oct. 1537, s. 28 Jan. 1547, d. 6 July 1553

Henry VIII m. 4, 6 Jan. 1539, Anne (b. 22 Sept. 1516, d. 17 July 1557) (marriage annulled 13 July 1540) d. of John, Duke of Cleves; m. 5, 8 Aug. 1540, Catharine (b.c. 1521, beheaded 13 Feb. 1542), d. of Lord Edmund Howard; m. 6, 12 July 1543 Katharine, (b. 1513. d.s.p. 5 Sept. 1548), d. of Sir Thomas Parr

Edmund, Duke of Somerset, b. 20 Feb. 1498, d. Jan. 1499

43. Henry VII

44. Henry VIII

45. Edward VI

47. Mary I

48. Elizabeth I

Margaret, b. 29 Nov. 1489, d. 18 Oct. 1541, m. 8 Aug. 1503 James IV, King of Scotland (k. at the battle of Flodden Field 9 Sept. 1513)

See Table 11—Kings of Scotland

Elizabeth, b. 2 July 1492, d. 14 Sept. 1495

Mary, b. 1498, d. 26 June 1533, m.1, 9 Oct. 1514, Louis XII, King of France (d.s.p. 1 Jan. 1515); she m. 2 as his 3rd wife, 13 May 1515, Charles Brandon, Duke of Suffolk (d. 14 Aug. 1545)

Henry, Earl of Lincoln, b. 11 March 1516, d. unm. 8 March 1534

Frances, b. 16 July 1517, d. 21 Nov. 1559, m.1, 1535, Henry Grey, 3rd Marquess of Dorset, later Duke of Suffolk (beheaded 23 Feb. 1554); she m. 2 Adrian Stokes (d.s.p.c. 1581)

Eleanor, b.c. 1520, d. Nov. 1547, m. 1537 Henry Clifford, 2nd Earl of Cumberland (d. 8 Jan. 1569)

issue, from whom descend the Earls of Derby

46. Jane† (commonly known as Lady Jane Grey), b. Oct. 1537, s. 6 July 1553 in accordance with the Wills of Henry VIII and Edward VI, dep. 19 July 1553, beheaded 12 Feb. 1553-4

Katherine, heiress presumptive to her sister, m.1., 21 May 1553 Henry Lord Herbert, later 2nd Earl of Pembroke; m. 2., Dec. 1560, Edward Seymour, 1st Earl of Hertford (d. 6 Apr. 1621) and d. a prisoner in the Tower of London 26 Jan. 1547

issue—heir-general Lady Kinloss

Mary, m. Aug. 1565 Thomas Keyes, from whom descend the Lords Keyes

† No mint

8 The House of Stewart

see page 34

49. James I of England, VI of Scotland, great-grandson of James IV of Scotland and his Queen Margaret, d. of **King Henry VII** (see Table 11—Kings of Scotland), b. 19 June 1566, King of Scotland from 24 June 1567, s. to throne of England 24 March 1603, d. 27 March 1625 m., 21 Nov. 1589, Anne (b. 14 Oct. 1574, d. 2 March 1618-19), d. of Frederick II, King of Denmark and Norway

Henry Frederick, Prince of Wales, b. 19 Feb. 1593-4, d. unm. 6 Nov. 1612

50. Charles I, b. 19 Nov. 1600, s. 27 March 1625, beheaded in Whitehall 30 Jan. 1649, m. 11 May 1625 Henrietta Maria (b. 25 Nov. 1609, d. 10 Sept. 1669), d. of Henry IV, King of France†

Robert, Duke of Kintyre, b. 18 Feb. 1601-2, d. unm. 27 May 1602

Charles James, Duke of Cornwall, b. and d. 13 May 1629

51. Charles II, b. 29 May 1630, s. 30 Jan. 1649, restored to the throne 29 May 1660, d. 6 Feb. 1685, m. 21 May 1662 Catherine of Braganza, Princess of Portugal (b. 25 Nov. 1638, d. 30 Nov. 1705), d. of John IV, King of Portugal

52. James II, b. 14 Oct. 1633, s. 6 Feb. 1685, deemed to have abdication on 11 Dec. 1688, d. 16 Sept. 1701, m.l, 24 Feb. 1659, Anne (b. 12 March 1637, d. 31 March 1671), d. of Earl of Clarendon; he m. 2, 21 Nov. 1673, Mary (b. 25 Sept. 1658, d. 8 May 1718), d. of Alphonso IV, Duke of Modena

Henry, Duke of Gloucester, b. 8 July, 1640, d. unm. 13 Sept. 1660

Mary, Princess Royal, b. 4 Nov. 1631, d. 24 Dec. 1660, m. 2 May 1648 William II, Prince of Orange (d. 6 Nov. 1650)

3ds d. young

4s., 2d. died young

54. Mary II, b. 30 Apr. 1662, s. with her husband **53. William III,** 13 Feb. 1689, d.s.p. 28 Dec. 1694

55. Anne, b. 6 Feb. 1655, s. 8 March 1702, d. 1 Aug. 1714, m. 28 July 1683 George, Prince of Denmark, s. of Frederick III, King of Denmark and Norway

issue, all of whom d. in childhood

James Francis Edward, 'The Old Pretender', b. 10 June 1688, d. 1 Jan. 1766, m. 28 May 1719 Mary Clementina (d. 30 Dec. 1735), d. of Prince James Sobieski

53. William III, Prince of Orange, b. posthumously 14 Nov. 1650, d.s.p. 8 March 1702, m. 4 Nov. 1677 his first cousin **54. Mary II,** with whom jointly he was summoned to the throne 13 Feb. 1689

Charles Edward Louis Philip Casimir, 'The Young Pretender', 'Bonnie Prince Charlie', b. 31 Dec. 1720, d.s.p. 31 Jan. 1788, m. 1772 Louisa Maximiliana (d. 29 Jan. 1824), d. of Gustavus Adolphus, Prince of Stolberg-Gedern

Henry Benedict Mary Clement (Cardinal Stewart 1747), b. 21 March 1725, d.s.p. 13 July 1807, when the representation of the line passed to Charles Emanuel IV, King of Sardinia (d.s.p. 6 Oct. 1819)

†Commonwealth 1649-1660
Oliver Cromwell, Commander-in-Chief March 1649; Protector 16 Dec. 1653; d. 3 Sept. 1658; Richard Cromwell, Protector 3 Sept. 1658-25 May 1659

49. James I

50. Charles I

51. Charles II

52. James II

Elizabeth, b. 19 Aug. 1596, d. 13 Feb. 1662, m. 14 Feb. 1613 Frederick V, Count Palatine of the Rhine, Elector, King of Bohemia (d. 29 Nov. 1632)

Margaret, b. 24 Dec. 1598, d. March 1600

Mary, b. 8 Apr. 1605, d. 16 Dec. 1607

Sophia, b. 22, d. 23 June 1606

Henrietta Anne, b. 16 June 1641, d. 30 June 1670, m. 31 March 1661 Philip Duke of Orleans (d. 9 June 1701)
issue
Dukes of Bavaria, present representatives of the Stewart lineage

Henry Frederick, King of Bohemia, b. 1 Jan. 1614, d. 7 Jan. 1628

Charles Lewis, Count Palatine, Elector, b. 12 Dec. 1617, d. 9 June 1701, m. 12 Feb. 1650 Charlotte (d. 26 March 1686), d. of William V, Landgrave of Hesse

Rupert 1, Count Palatine, Duke of Cumberland, b. 17 Dec. 1619, d. unm. 29 Nov. 1682

2s.

Sophia, b. 13 Oct. 1630, d. 8 June 1714, declared heir presumptive to England, Ireland and Scotland 6 March 1701-2, m. 30 Sept. 1658 Ernest Augustus, Duke of Brunswick and Lüneberg, King of Hanover, Elector (d. 23 Jan. 1698)

4d.

56. George I
See Table 9 —House of Hanover

continued on page 24

Frederick Augustus, b. 3 Oct. 1661, k. in battle against the Turks, unm., 30 Dec. 1690

Maximilian William, b. 23 Dec. 1666, d. unm. 16 July 1726

Charles Philip, b. 13 Oct. 1669, k. in battle against the Turks 1 Jan. 1690-1, unm.

Christian, b. 19 Sept. 1671, d. by drowning 31 July 1703, unm.

Ernest Augustus, Duke of York and Albany, b. 7 Sept. 1674, d. unm. 14 Aug. 1728

Sophia Charlotte, b. 20 Oct. 1668, d. 21 Jan. 1705, m. 6 Oct. 1684 Frederick I, King of Prussia
issue

53, 54. William III and Mary II

55. Anne

9 The House of Hanover

continued from page 23

56. George I, b. 28 May 1660 (Georg Ludvig, Duke of Brunswick-Lüneberg), Elector of Hanover, s. 1 Aug. 1714, d. 11 June 1727, m. 21 Nov. 1682 (diss. 28 Dec. 1694) his first cousin Sophia Dorothea (b. 3 Feb. 1666, d. 13 Nov. 1726), d. of George William, Duke of Brunswick-Zell

57. George II Augustus, b. 30 Oct. 1683, s. 11 June 1727, d. 25 Oct. 1760, m. Caroline (b. 1 March 1682, d. 20 Nov. 1737), d. of John Frederick, Margrave of Brandenburg-Anspach

Frederick Lewis, Prince of Wales, b. 20 Jan. 1707, d. 20 March 1751, m. 27 Apr. 1736 Augusta (b. 30 Nov. 1719, d. 8 Feb. 1772), d. of Frederick II, Duke of Saxe-Gotha-Altenburg

George William, b. 3 Nov. 1717, d. 6 Feb. 1718

William Augustus, Duke of Cumberland, 'Butcher Cumberland', b. 15 Apr. 1721, d. unm. 31 Oct. 1765

Anne, Princess Royal, b. 2 Nov. 1709, d. 12 Jan. 1759, m. 25 March 1734 William IV, Prince of Orange-Nassau-Dietz (d. 22 Oct. 1751)
issue

58. George III, b. 4 June 1738, s. 25 Oct. 1760, d. 29 Jan. 1820, m. 8 Sept. 1761 Sophia Charlotte, (b. 19 May 1744, d. 17 Nov. 1818), d. of Charles I, Duke of Mecklenburg-Strelitz

Edward Augustus, Duke of York and Albany, Earl of Ulster, b. 14 March 1739, d. unm. 7 Sept. 1767

William Henry, 1st Duke of Gloucester and Edinburgh, Earl of Connaught, b. 14 Nov. 1743, d. 25 Aug. 1805, m. 6 Sept. 1766 Maria (d. 22 Aug. 1807) widow of James, 2nd Earl Waldegrave, and illeg. d. of the Hon. Sir Edward Walpole
issue

Henry Frederick, Duke of Cumberland and Strathearn, b. 27 Oct. 1745, d.s.p. 18 Sept. 1790, m. 2 Oct. 1771 Anne (d. 28 Dec. 1808), widow of Christopher Horton and d. of Simon Luttrell, 1st Earl of Carhampton

59. George IV, b. 12 Aug. 1762, Prince Regent from 5 Feb. 1811, s. 29 Jan. 1820, d. 26 June 1830, m. 8 Apr. 1795 Caroline Amelia Elizabeth (b. 1768, d. 7 Aug. 1821), d. of Charles William, Duke of Mecklenburg-Strelitz

Frederick Augustus, Duke of York and Albany, b. 16 Aug. 1783, d. s.p. 5 Jan. 1827, m. 1791 Frederica Charlotte Ulrica Catherine (d. 6 Aug. 1820), d. of Frederick William II, King of Prussia

60. William IV b. 21 Aug. 1765, s. 26 June 1830, d. 20 June 1837, m. 11 July 1818 Adelaide (b. 14 Aug. 1792, d. 2 Dec. 1849), d. of George I, Duke of Saxe-Meiningen
2d.—d. in infancy

Edward Augustus, Duke of Kent, b. 2 Nov. 1767, d. 23 Jan. 1820, m. 20 May 1818 Victoria Mary Louise (d. 16 March 1861), widow of Emich Charles, Prince of Leiningen, d. of Francis Frederick Antony, Duke of Saxe-Saalfeld-Coburg

Ernest Augustus, Duke of Brunswick-Lüneburg, King of Hanover, b. 5 June 1771, d. 18 Nov. 1851, m. 29 May 1815 Frederica (d. 29 June 1841) d. of Charles Louis Frederick, Grand Duke of Mecklenburg-Strelitz
issue

Augustus Frederick, Duke of Sussex, b. 27 Jan. 1773, d.s.p. 21 Apr. 1843, m. 4 Apr. 1793 in violation of the Royal Marriage Act, 1772, Lady Augusta Murray (d. 5 March 1830); m. 2, May 1831, again violating the Royal Marriage Act, Lady Cecilia Letitia Buggin (later Underwood), created Duchess of Inverness 1840 (d. 1 Aug. 1873)

Charlotte Augusta, b. 7 Jan. 1796, d.s.p. 6 Nov. 1817, m. 2 May 1816 Prince Leopold of Saxe-Saalfeld-Coburg, elected Leopold I, King of the Belgians 4 June 1831 (d. 10 Dec. 1865)

61. Victoria, b. 24 May 1819, s. 20 June 1837, d. 22 Jan. 1901, m. 10 Feb. 1840 Prince Albert of Saxe-Coburg and Gotha (b. 26 Aug. 1819, d. 14 Dec. 1861), created Prince Consort 25 June 1857

see page 26

56. George I

Sophia Dorothea, b. 16 March 1685, d. 29 June 1757, m. 28 Nov. 1706 Frederick William I, King of Prussia
issue

Amelia Sophia Eleanor, b. 10 June 1711, d. unm. 31 Oct. 1786

Caroline Elizabeth, b. 10 June 1713, d. unm. 28 Dec. 1757

Mary, b. 22 Feb. 1723, d. 14 Jan. 1772, m. as 1st wife 8 May 1740 Frederick II, Landgrave of Hesse-Cassel
issue

Louisa, b. 7 Dec. 1724, d. 8 Dec. 1751, m. as 1st wife Frederick V, King of Denmark and Norway
issue

Frederick William, b. 13 May 1750, d. 29 Dec. 1765

Augusta, b. 31 July 1737, d. 23 March 1813, m. 17 Jan. 1764 Charles William Ferdinand, Duke of Brunswick-Wölfenbuttell
issue

Elizabeth Caroline, b. 30 Dec. 1740, d. 4 Sept. 1759

Louisa Ann, b. 8 March 1748-9, d. unm. 13 May 1768

Caroline Matilda, b. 11 July 1751, d. 10 May 1775, m. 1 Oct. 1766 Christian VII, King of Denmark and Norway
issue

Adolphus Frederick, 1st Duke of Cambridge, b. 24 Feb. 1774, d. 8 July 1850, m. 7 May 1818 Augusta Wilhelmina Louise (d. 6 Apr. 1889), d. of Frederick, Landgrave of Hesse-Cassel, leaving issue (from whom descended Queen Mary, wife of King George V)

2s. d. young

Charlotte Augusta Matilda, Princess Royal, b. 29 Sept. 1766, d.s.p. 6 Oct. 1828, m. 18 May 1797 Frederick I, King of Württemburg (d. 30 Oct. 1816)

Augusta Sophia, b. 8 Nov. 1768, d. unm. 22 Sept. 1840

Elizabeth, b. 22 May 1770, d.s.p. 10 Jan. 1840, m. 7 Apr. 1818 Frederick, Landgrave of Hesse-Homburg (d. 2 Apr. 1829)

Mary, b. 25 Apr. 1776, d.s.p. 30 Apr. 1857, m. 22 July 1816 her first cousin, William Frederick, 2nd Duke of Gloucester (d. 30 Nov. 1834)

Sophia, b. 3 Nov. 1777, d. unm. 27 May 1848

Amelia, b. 7 Aug. 1783, d. unm. 2 Nov. 1810

57. George II

58. George III

59. George IV

60. William IV

61. Victoria

continued from page 24

62. Edward VII, b. 9 Nov. 1841, s. 22 Jan. 1901, d. 6 May 1910, m. 10 March 1863 PrincessAlexandra, (b. 1 Dec. 1844, d. 20 Nov. 1925), d. of Christian IX, King of Denmark

Alfred Ernest Albert, Duke of Saxe-Coburg and Gotha, b. 6 Aug. 1844, d. 30 July 1900, m. 23 Jan. 1874 Grand Duchess Marie (d. 25 Oct. 1920), d. of Alexander II, Tsar of Russia

issue, including Royal Houses of Roumania, Russia and Yugoslavia

Arthur William Patrick Albert, 1st Duke of Connaught, b. 1 May 1850, d. 16 Jan. 1942, m. 13 March 1879 Princess Louise (d. 14 March 1917), d. of Prince Frederick Charles of Prussia

issue, including the Royal House of Sweden and the Earls of Dalhousie

Leopold George Duncan Albert, 1st Duke of Albany, b. 7 Apr. 1853, d. 28 March 1884, m. 27 Apr. 1882 Princess Helen Frederica Augusta (d. 1 Sept. 1922), d. of George Victor, Prince of Waldeck and Pyrmont

issue—
Dukes of Saxony

Albert Victor Christian Edward, Duke of Clarence and Avondale, b. 8 Jan. 1864, d. unm. 14 Jan. 1892

63. George V
See Table 10 —House of Windsor, p. 28

Alexander John Charles Albert, b. 6 Apr. 1871, d. 7 Apr. 1871

Louise Victoria Alexandra Dagmar, Princess Royal, b. 20 Feb. 1867, d. 4 Jan. 1931, m. 27 July 1889 1st Duke of Fife (d. 29 Jan. 1912)

issue—Dukes of Fife

62. Edward VII

Victoria Adelaide Mary Louisa, Princess Royal, b. 21 Nov. 1840, d. 5 Aug. 1901, m. 25 Jan. 1858 Frederick, later King of Prussia and German Emperor (d. 1888)

issue—Royal Houses of Hohenzollern and Greece

Alice Maud Mary, b. 25 Apr. 1843, d. 14 Dec. 1878, m. 1 July 1862 Louis IV, Grand Duke of Hesse (d. 13 March 1892)

issue*—including the Imperial Family of Russia

Helena Augusta Victoria, b. 25 May 1846, d. 9 June 1923, m. 5 July 1866, Prince Christian of Schleswig-Holstein (d. 28 Oct. 1917)

issue

Louise Caroline Alberta, b. 18 March 1848, d.s.p. 3 Dec. 1939, m. 21 March 1871 9th Duke of Argyll (d. 2 May 1914)

Beatrice Mary Victoria Feodore, b. 14 May 1857, d. 26 Oct. 1944, m. 23 July 1885 Prince Henry of Battenberg (d. 20 Jan. 1896)

issue—including Royal House of Spain

Victoria Alexandra Olga Mary, b. 6 July 1868; d. unm. 3 Dec. 1935

Maud Charlotte Mary Victoria, b. 26 Nov. 1869, d. 20 Nov. 1938, m. 22 July 1896 her first cousin, later King Haakon VII of Norway (d. 21 Sept. 1957)

issue—Royal House of Norway

* Their d. Princess Victoria m. Louis Alexander, Prince of Battenburg, later 1st Marquess of Milford Haven, by whom she had two s., George, 2nd Marquess of Milford Haven, and Louis, 1st Earl Mountbatten of Burma, and one d., Alice, m. Prince Andrew of Greece, whose son, Philip, Duke of Edinburgh m. **H.M. Queen Elizabeth.**

10 The House of Windsor

continued from page 26

63. George V (George Frederick Ernest Albert), b. 3 June 1865, Duke of York 1892, Prince of Wales 1901, s. 6 May 1910, d. 20 Jan. 1936, m. Princess Mary, only d. of the Duke of Teck (b. 26 May 1867, d. 24 March 1953)

64. Edward VIII, b. 23 June 1894, s. 20 Jan. 1936, abdicated 10 Dec. 1936, created Duke of Windsor 8 March 1937, d. 28 May 1972, m. 3 June 1937 Wallis (formerly Simpson), d. of Teakle Wallis Warfield

65. George VI, b. 14 Dec. 1895, s. 10 Dec. 1936, d. 6 Feb. 1952, m. 26 Apr. 1923. Lady Elizabeth Angela Marguerite Bowes-Lyon (b. 4 Aug. 1900). d. of 14th Earl of Strathmore & Kinghorne (H.M. QUEEN ELIZABETH THE QUEEN MOTHER)

66. HER MAJESTY QUEEN ELIZABETH II (Elizabeth Alexandra Mary), s. 6 Feb. 1952, b. 21 Apr. 1926, m. 20 Nov. 1947 H.R.H. Prince Philip, Duke of Edinburgh (see Table 9) (b. 10 June 1921)

Princess Margaret (Rose) b. 21 Aug. 1930, m. 6 May 1960 Anthony Armstrong Jones, cr. 1st Earl of Snowdon 1961

David Albert Charles, Viscount Linley, b. 3 Nov. 1961

Sarah Frances Elizabeth, b. 1 May 1964

H.R.H. Prince Charles, Prince of Wales, b. 14 Nov. 1948

H.R.H. Prince Andrew, b. 19 Feb. 1960

H.R.H. Prince Edward, b. 10 March 1964

H.R.H. Princess Anne, b. 15 Aug. 1950, m., 14 Nov. 1973, Captain Mark Anthony Peter Phillips (b. 22 Sept. 1948), son of P. W. G. Phillips

63. George V

64. Edward VIII

65. George VI

66. Elizabeth II

lenry William Frederick
lbert, Duke of Gloucester,
. 31 March 1900, d. 10 June
974, m. 6 Nov. 1935 Lady
lice Christabel Montagu-
ouglas-Scott, d. of 7th
uke of Buccleuch

George Edward Alexander
Edmund, Duke of Kent, b. 20
Dec. 1902, k. in an aircraft
accident while on active service
25 Aug. 1942, m. 29 Nov.
1934. H.R.H. Princess Marina,
(d. 27 Aug. 1968) d. of
Prince Nicholas of Greece

John
Charles
Francis,
b. 12 July
1905; d.
18 Jan.
1919

Victoria Alexandra
Alice Mary, Princess
Royal, b. 25 Apr. 1897,
d. 28 March 1965, m. 28
Feb. 1922 6th Earl of
Harewood (d. 24 May 1947)

'illiam Henry
ndrew Frederick,
. 18 Aug. 1941,
. in an
ircraft accident
8 Aug. 1972

Richard Alexander
Walter George, 2nd Duke
of Gloucester, b. 26
Aug. 1944, m. 8
July 1972 Birgette
Eva, d. of Asger
Proben Wissing
Henriksen, and his
first wife Vivian,
d. of Waldemar
Oswald van Deurs

Alexander Patrick
Gregers Richard,
Earl of Ulster,
b. 24 Oct. 1974

Edward George
Nicholas Paul
Patrick, 2nd
Duke of Kent,
b. 9 Oct. 1935,
m. 8 June 1961
Katharine Lucy
Mary, d. of
Sir William
Worsley

George Philip
Nicholas, Earl
of St Andrews,
b. 26 June 1962

Nicholas Charles
Edward Jonathan,
b. 25 July 1970

Helen
Marina
Lucy,
b. 28 Apr.
1964

Michael George
Charles Franklin,
b. 4 July 1942

Alexandra Helen
Elizabeth Olga
Christabel, b.
25 Dec. 1936, m.
Angus James
Bruce Ogilvy, 2nd
son of (12th) Earl
of Airlie

James Robert
Bruce,
b. 29 Feb. 1964

Marina Victoria
Alexandra,
b. 31 July 1966

ieorge Henry Hubert,
th Earl of Harewood,
. 7 Feb. 1923, m.1, 29
ept. 1949 (diss. 1967),
laria (Marion), d. of
rwin Stein

avid Henry George,
'iscount Lascelles,
. 21 Oct. 1950

James Edward,
b. 5 Oct. 1953,
m. 1973
Fredericka
Ann Durrhssen

Sophie Amber
b. 1 Oct. 1973

Robert Jeremy
Hugh, b. 14
Feb. 1955

ord Harewood m.2,
1 July 1967,
'atricia Elizabeth,
. of Charles
'uckwell

lark Hubert,
. 5 July 1964

Gerald David,
b. 21 Aug. 1924,
m. 15 July 1952,
Angela, d. of Charles
Stanley Dowding

Henry Ulick,
b. 19 May 1953

11 Kings of Scotland

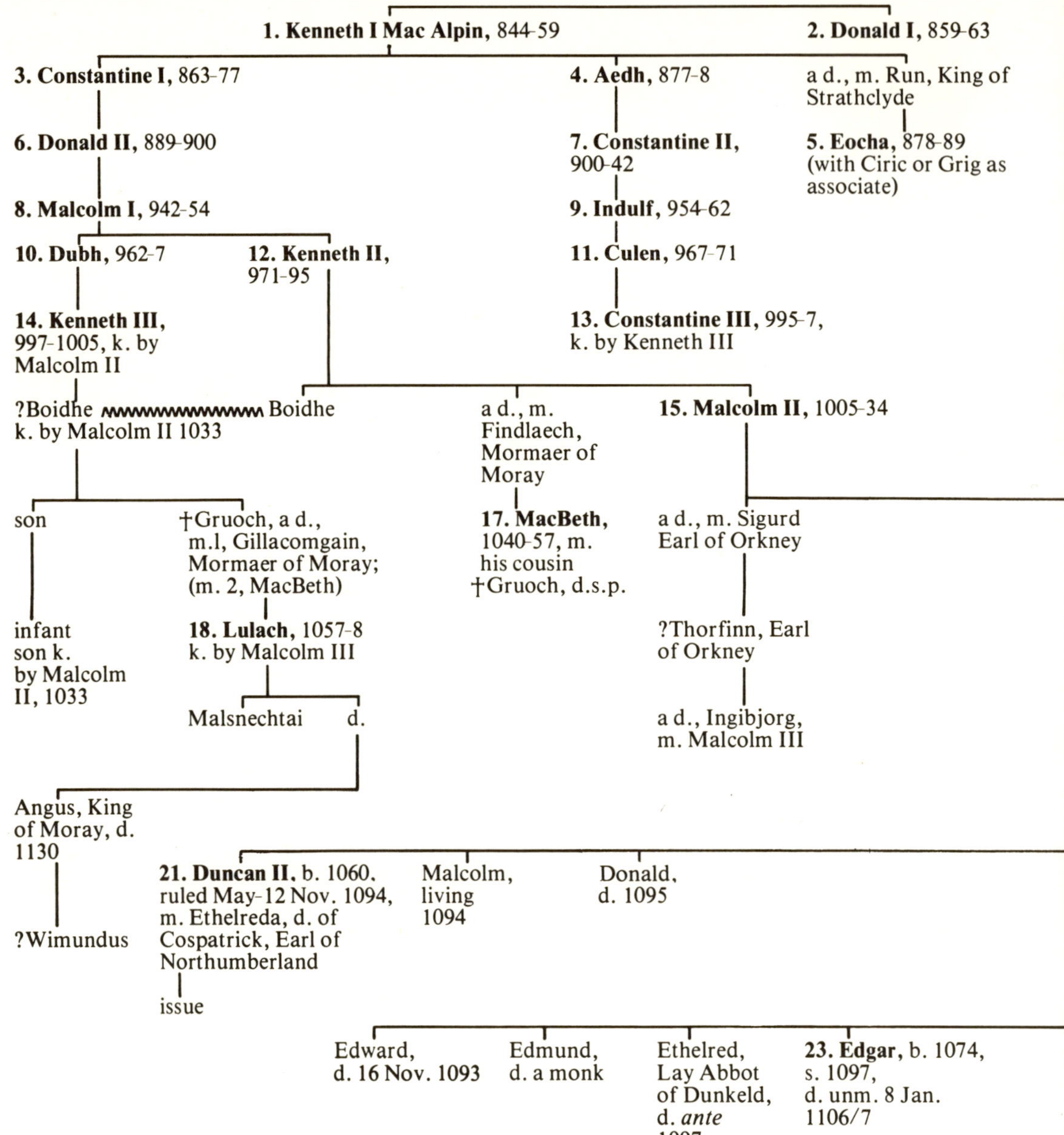

†Shakespeare's 'Lady Macbeth'.

25. David I

Bethoc, m. Crinan of Dunkeld

16. Duncan I, 1034-40, k. by Macbeth

19. Malcolm III, b.c., 1031, 1058-93, m.1, his first cousin Ingibjorg; he m. 2, 1068, Saint Margaret (d. 16 Nov. 1093, canonized 1250), d. of Edward the Exile (see Table 2, p. 3)

20, 22. Donald Bane, ruled 13 Nov. 1093 May 1094; dep. by Duncan II; restored 12 Nov. 1094; dep. 1097. For his descendant John Comyn, who claimed the throne in 1291, see below, p. 33

24. Alexander I, b. 1077, s. 1107, d. 1124, m. Sybilla (d.s.p. 12 July 1122), illeg. d. of Henry I, King of England

25. David I ('The Saint'), b.c. 1080, s. 1124, d. 1153, m.c. 1114 Matilda, widow of Simon de Senlis or St Liz, d. and heiress of Waltheof, Earl of Huntingdon (see p. 9)

Eadgith, or Matilda, m. 11 Nov. 1100, Henry I, King of England—see Table 3

Mary, m. 1102 Eustace, Count of Boulogne, and d. 31 May 1116

issue

Malcolm, strangled as a child by Donald Bane

Henry, Earl of Huntingdon, d. 12 June 1152, m. 1139, name not known, d. of William de Warenne, Earl of Surrey

See pages 32-3

Claricia d. unm.

Hodierna d. unm.

continued from page 31

26. Malcolm IV ('The Maiden'), b. 20 March 1141–2, s. 1153, d. unm. 9 Dec. 1165

27. William ('The Lion'), b.c. 1143, s. 9 Dec. 1165, d. 4 Dec. 1214, m. 5 Sept. 1186 Ermengarde (d. 11 Feb. 1233–4), d. of Richard, Viscount of Bellemont;

he had illegitimately

28. Alexander II, b. 24 Aug. 1198, s. 4 Dec. 1214, d. 8 July 1249, m.1, Joan (d.s.p. 4 March 1237–8), d. of John, King of England; m. 2, 15 May 1239, Mary, d. of Enguerand, Seigneur de Couci

Margaret, d.s.p. 1295, m. 1221 Hubert de Burgh, Earl of Kent

Isabella, m. 1225 Roger Bigod, Earl of Norfolk (d.s.p. 4 July 1270)

Marjory, d.s.p. 17 Nov. 1244, m. 1 Aug. 1235 Gilbert, Earl of Pembroke (d. *post* 27 June 1241)

Isabella — William Ros (1) — Robert Ros — †William Ros (2)

Ada, m. 5th Earl of Dunbar — Patric, 6th Earl — Patric, 7th Earl — †Patric, 8th Earl, 1st Earl of March

Margaret — William de Vesci (1) — †William de Vesci (2)

29. Alexander III, b. 4 Sept. 1241, s. 8 July 1249, d. 19 March 1285–6, m.1, Margaret (d. 26 Feb. 1274–5), d. of Henry III, King of England;

he m. 2, Yolande, d. of Robert IV, Count of Dreux

he had illeg. Marjory, m. Alan Durward the Justiciary — Ermengarde — †Nicholas Soules

Alexander, b. 21 Jan. 1263–4, d.s.p. 28 Jan. 1283–4, m. 15 Nov. 1282, Margaret, d. of Guy of Flanders

David, b. 20 March 1272–3, d. unm. June 1281

30, Margaret* 'The b. 28 Feb. 1260–1, d. 9 Apr. 1283, m. 31 Aug. 1281, Eric Magnusson,† King of Norway (d. 1299)

30, Margaret* 'The Maid of Norway', b. *ante* 9 Apr. 1283, d. unm. 26 Sept. 1290

†The twelve competitors for the throne in 1290–2 as submitted to the arbitration of King Edward I of England. These included claimants of illegitimate descent, in accordance with Scottish law.

*No mint

26. Malcolm IV

27. William the Lion

28. Alexander II

29. Alexander III

31. John Baliol

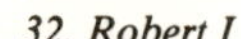

32. Robert I

33. David II

34. Robert II

David, Earl of Huntington, d. 17 June 1219, m. 26 Aug. 1190 Maud, d. of Hugh de Kevilloc, Earl of Chester

Aufrica — William — Aufrica — Agatha — †Roger de Mandeville

Henry Galithly — †Patrick Galithly

Ada, m. 1161 Florent III, Count of Holland — William I — Florent IV — William II — †Florent V, Count of Holland

Margaret, m.1, Conan, Duke of Brittany, Earl of Richmond (d. 20 Feb. 1170–1) — Constance, m. Geoffrey, s. of Henry II, King of England; she m.2 Humphrey de Bohun, Earl of Hereford

Matilda, d. young 1152

DESCENDANTS OF DONALD BANE

Bethoc (2) — Hextilda — William Comyn — Richard Comyn — John Comyn of Badenoch (1) — †John Comyn (2), m. sister of John Baliol — John Comyn (3) ('Red Comyn'), k. by Robert the Bruce

Children of David, Earl of Huntington:

2s. 1d. unm.

John ('The Scot'), Earl of Chester and Huntingdon, d.s.p. 5 June 1237

Margaret, m. 1209 Alan, Lord of Galloway (d. 1234)

Isabella, m. Robert Bruce, Lord of Allandale (d. 1245)

Matilda d. unm.

Ada m. Henry de Hastings — Sir Henry de Hastings — †John, 1st Lord Hastings

Children of Margaret and Alan of Galloway:

Helen, m. Roger de Quincey, Earl of Winchester, (d. 1264) — issue

Christian d.s.p. 1245–6, m. 1236 William, Earl of Albemarle

Dervorguilla d. 28 Jan. 1289–90, m. 1233 John Baliol (d. 1269)

Children of Isabella and Robert Bruce:

†Robert, d. *ante* 3 May 1294, m. Isabel, d. of Gilbert de Clare, Earl of Gloucester and Hereford

Beatrice, m. Hugo de Neville

Children of Robert and Isabel:

Robert Bruce, Earl of Carrick *jure uxoris*, m. 1271 Margaret, d. of 2nd Earl of Carrick

3s

Children of Dervorguilla and John Baliol:

3s.

†**31. John Baliol**, b.c. 1250, d.c. Apr. 1313, crowned, following award of Edward I of England, 30 Nov. 1292, dep. 10 July 1296, m. *ante* 7 Feb. 1280–1 Isabel, d. of John de Warenne, Earl of Surrey

2d.

Children of John Baliol:

Edward, crowned by the English at Scone 24 Sept. 1332; fled Scotland 1332; d.s.p. 1363

Henry, k. 16 Dec. 1332

Children of Robert Bruce, Earl of Carrick:

32. Robert I 'The Bruce', b. 11 July 1274, d. 7 June 1329, crowned King of Scotland 27 March 1306, re-established independence of Scotland following Edward I's subjugation (1296–1314) at the battle of Bannockburn, m.1, Isabel, d. of Donald, 6th Earl of Mar; he m.2, 1302, Elizabeth de Burgh (d. 26 Oct. 1327), d. of Richard, Earl of Ulster

Edward, Earl of Carrick, King of Ireland 2 May 1316, k. at battle of Dundalk 14 Oct. 1318 s.p.

3s, 5d

Child of Robert I by 1st marriage:

Marjorie, d. 2 March 1315–16, m. 1315 Walter the Stewart, 6th High Steward of Scotland

34. Robert II (first King of the House of Stewart), b. 2 March 1315–16, s. 22 Feb. 1370–1, d. 19 Apr. 1390, m.1, Elizabeth (d. *ante* 1355), d. of Sir Adam Mure; he m.2, 1355, Euphemia (d. 1387), widow of John Randolph, Earl of Moray, d. of Hugh, Earl of Ross

See page 35

Children of Robert I by 2nd marriage:

33. David II, b. 5 March 1323–4, s. 7 June 1329. d.s.p. 22 Feb. 1370–1, m.1, Joan (d.s.p. 7 Sept. 1362), d. of Edward II, King of England; m. 2, 20 Feb. 1363–4, Margaret (div. 20 March 1369–70, d.c. 31 Jan. 1374–5), widow of Sir John Logie and d. of Sir Malcolm Drummond

John, d. young

Matilda, d. 20 July 1353, m. Thomas Isaac

Margaret, d. 1358, m. *ante* 10 Nov. 1345 5th Earl of Sutherland

35. Robert III, b. 1337, s. 19 Apr. 1390, d. 4 Apr. 1406, m. Annabella, (d. 1401), d. of John Drummond of Stobhall

Walter d.s.p. *post* 14 Aug. 1362, m. Isabel, Countess of Fife

Robert, 1st Duke of Albany, b.c. 1340, d. 3 Sept. 1420, m.1, 9 Sept. 1361, Margaret, Countess of Menteith (d. 1380) and had issue; m. 2. Muriella (d. 1449), d. of Sir William Keith and had issue

Alexander, Earl of Buchan ('The Wolf of Badenoch'), d.s.p. 24 July 1394, m. Euphaemia, Countess of Ross

Margaret, m. 14 June 1350 John Macdonald, Lord of the Isles (d. 1387)
issue

Marjorie, m.1, c. 11 July 1371, John Dunbar, Earl of Moray (d.c. 1390, leaving issue); m. 2, c. 1403, Sir Alexander Keith

---

David, Earl of Carrick, Duke of Rothesay, b. 24 Oct. 1378, d.s.p. 26 March 1402, m. Feb. 1399–1400 Marjorie, d. of Archibald, 3rd Earl of Douglas

Robert, d. young

36. James I, b. Dec. 1394, s. 4 Apr. 1406, assassinated 21 Feb. 1436–7, m. 2 Feb. 1423–4, Lady Joan Beaufort (d. 15 July 1445), d. of 1st Earl of Somerset

Margaret, m. Archibald, 4th Earl of Douglas, Duke of Touraine
issue

Mary, d. 1458, m.1, 1397, George, Earl of Angus; m. 2, 1404, Sir James Kennedy of Dunmure; m.3, 1413, William, 1st Lord Graham; m. 4, 1425, Sir William Edmonstone of Duntreath, and had issue by all four

Egidia

Alexander, b. 16 Oct. 1430, d. an infant

37. James II, b. 16 Oct. 1430, s. 21 Feb. 1436–7, k. by a piece of ordnance bursting at Roxburgh Castle 3 Aug. 1460, m. 3 July 1449 Mary (d. 1 Dec. 1463), d. of Arnold, Duke of Gueldres

Margaret, d.s.p. 16 Aug. 1444, m. 24 June 1436 Louis, Dauphin of France, later King Louis XI

Isabella, d. 1494, m. 30 Oct. 1442 Francis, Duke of Brittany
issue

---

38. James III, b. 10 July 1451, s. 3 Aug. 1460, d. 11 June 1488, m. 13 July 1469 Margaret (d. 14 July 1486), d. of Christian I, King of Denmark

Alexander, Duke of Albany, d. 1485, m.1, (diss. 1478) Lady Katharine Sinclair, d. of William, Earl of Caithness; m.2, 19 Jan. 1479–80, Anne, d. of Bertrand de la Tour, Count of Auvergne
issue

---

39. James IV, b. 17 March 1472–3, s. 11 June 1488, k. at battle of Flodden Field 9 Sept. 1513, m. Margaret, d. of Henry VII of England (see Table 7)

James, b. March 1475–6 d. unm. Jan. 1502–3

John, created Earl of Mar, b. 2 March 1486–7, d. unm. 11 March 1502–3

James, b. 21 Feb. 1506–7, d. 27 Feb. 1507–8

Arthur, b. 20 Oct. 1509, d. 14 July 1510

40. James V, b. 10 Apr. 1512, s. 9 Sept. 1513, d. 14 Dec. 1542, m.1, 1 Jan. 1536–7, Madeline de Valois (d.s.p. 7 July 1537), d. of Francis I, King of France; m. 2, June 1538, Marie de Lorraine (d. 10 June 1560), d. of Claude de Guise Lorraine, Duke of Aumale, Regent of Scotland during her d.'s minority

41. Mary, Queen of Scots, b. 7 or 8 Dec. 1542, s. 14 Dec. 1542, compelled to abdicate 24 July 1567, executed 8 Feb. 1586–7, m.1, 24 Apr. 1558, Francis, Dauphin of France, later King Francis II (d.s.p. 5 Dec. 1560); m.2, 29 July 1565, her cousin Henry, Lord Darnley, created Duke of Albany, Earl of Ross (murdered 10 Feb. 1566–7)

42. James VI, b. 19 June 1566, s. 24 July 1567, and s. his cousin Elizabeth as King of England, 24 March 1603—see Table 8—House of Stewart continued from page 33

Jean, m.1, Sir John Keith; m. 2, 1379, Sir John Lyon, ancestor of the Earls of Strathmore; m. 3, Sir James Sandilands of Calder, ancestor of the Lords Torphichen

Isabella, m.1, c. 1371, 2nd Earl of Douglas (d.s.p. 19 Aug. 1388); m.2, *ante* 1390, Sir John Edmonstone
issue

Elizabeth, m. *ante* 7 Nov. 1372 Sir Thomas Hay, Lord the Hay, Constable of Scotland, from whom descend the Earls of Erroll

continued from page 33

David, Earl Palatine of Strathearn, Earl of Caithness, b.c. 1356, d. *ante* 1389
issue

Walter, Earl of Caithness, m. *ante* 19 Oct. 1378 Margaret, d. and heiress of Sir David de Barclay, Lord of Brechin, and was executed and attainted 26 March 1437
issue

Egidia, m. 1387 Sir William Douglas of Nithsdale, illeg. s. of Archibald, 3rd Earl of Douglas
issue

Katherine (or Jean, or Elizabeth), m. 1380 Sir David Lindsay, 1st Earl of Crawford, from whom descend the Earls of Crawford and Balcarres

Elizabeth, m. 1387 James, Lord of Dalkeith, grandfather of 1st Earl of Moreton

35. *Robert III*

36. *James I*

Joanna (both deaf and dumb), m. *ante* 15 May 1459 1st Earl of Morton, from whom descend the Earls of Morton

Eleanor, d.s.p. 4 March 1496, m. 12 Feb. 1449 Sigismund, Duke of Austria

Mary, m. 1444 Wolfaert von Borselen, Count of Grandpré

Annabella, m.1, 14 Dec. 1447 (div.) Louis, Count of Geneva, s. of Duke of Savoy; m. 2, *ante* 10 March 1459 (div. 24 July 1471), George, Earl of Huntly

David, d. an infant *ante* 18 July 1457

John, Earl of Mar, b. 1459, d. unm. 1479

Mary, d. May 1488, m.1, *ante* 26 Apr. 1467, Thomas Boyd, Earl of Arran (d. c. 1474), leaving issue; m.2, *ante* Apr. 1474, James, 1st Lord Hamilton, from whom descend the Dukes of Abercorn

Margaret, d. unm.

m. 3, 15 May 1567, 4th Earl of Bothwell, created Duke of Orkney (d.s.p. 14 Apr. 1578)

37. *James II*

38. *James III*

39. *James IV*

40. *James V*

41. *Mary*

42. *James VI*

INDEX